Overcoming Trauma Through Yoga

Reclaiming Your Body

David Emerson
Elizabeth Hopper, PhD
Forewords By Peter A. Levine, Phd, And
Stephen Cope, MSW
Introduction By Bessel A. Van Der Kolk, MD

16pt

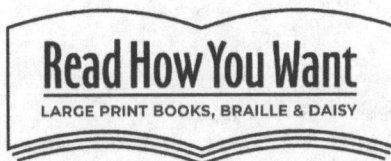
Read How You Want
LARGE PRINT BOOKS, BRAILLE & DAISY

Copyright Page from the Original Book

Published by

North Atlantic Books	and	The Trauma Center at Justice Resource Institute, Inc.
P.O. Box 12327		545 Boylston St., Suite 700
Berkeley, California 94712		Boston, MA 02116

Cover photo © iStockphoto.com/Peter Zelei
Cover and book design by Claudia Smelser
Printed in the United States of America

Overcoming Trauma through Yoga: Reclaiming Your Body is sponsored by the Society for the Study of Native Arts and Sciences, a nonprofit educational corporation whose goals are to develop an educational and cross-cultural perspective linking various scientific, social, and artistic fields; to nurture a holistic view of arts, sciences, humanities, and healing; and to publish and distribute literature on the relationship of mind, body, and nature. This book is co-sponsored by the Trauma Center, a national expert research, training, and service center dedicated to unraveling the complex effects of psychological trauma and developing state-of-the-art treatment for impacted children and adults. The Trauma Center is a program of Justice Resource Institute, a nonprofit organization whose mission is to pursue social justice through empowering underserved individuals and communities through cultivation of strength, well-being, and autonomy.

North Atlantic Books' publications are available through most bookstores. For further information, visit our website at www.northatlanticbooks.com or call 800-733-3000.

The Trauma Center offers a wide range of educational materials for survivors of traumatic events and multidisciplinary service providers. For further information, visit our website at www.traumacenter.org or call 617-232-1303.

MEDICAL DISCLAIMER: The following information is intended for general information purposes only. Individuals should always see their health care provider before administering any suggestions made in this book. Any application of the material set forth in the following pages is at the reader's discretion and is his or her sole responsibility.

Library of Congress Cataloging-in-Publication Data

Emerson, David, 1969–
Overcoming trauma through yoga: reclaiming your body / David Emerson, Elizabeth Hopper.
    p. cm.
SBN 978-1-55643-969-8
1. Psychic trauma—Physical therapy. 2. Yoga—Therapeutic use. I. Hopper, Elizabeth, 1973– II. Title.
RC552.T7E44 2010
616.85'2106—dc22

2010030105

3 4 5 6 7 8 9 10 Sheridan 16 15 14 13 12 11

TABLE OF CONTENTS

We would like to dedicate this book to survivors of trauma everywhere.

Acknowledgments

I would like to thank Richard Grossinger and Lindy Hough at North Atlantic Books for being so kind and generous and for believing in our topic. I would also like to thank Jessica Sevey specifically along with everyone else at North Atlantic Books who had a hand in this final product—what a fantastic, patient, and professional group! Thanks to Dana Moore, Jodi Carey, and Jenn Turner for their specific contributions to the development of the Trauma Center Yoga Program and to all of the other wonderful yoga teachers who have been involved with the program. Deep gratitude to Bessel A. van der Kolk for being a champion of yoga in the field of trauma and for being somebody whom I am proud to call "teacher." To everyone at the Trauma Center, Joseph Spinazzola, Margaret Blaustein, and Ritu Sharma in particular, thank you for supporting me and nurturing the yoga program with your tremendous intelligence and generosity. Finally, thank you to my family, especially Mandy and Hazen, and to my friends for supporting me throughout the writing process and for giving me a reason to get up each day.

David Emerson

I would like to thank my mentors and colleagues at the Trauma Center for guiding and supporting my learning about trauma treatment, and for giving me my professional home. Thanks to Dave for his calm presence, enthusiasm, and kind spirit in his leadership of our yoga program. Thank you to the therapists and yoga instructors who have attended our workshops, and to the women and men who have attended our yoga classes, for generously sharing their own experiences and giving us much food for thought. Many thanks to our executive director, Joseph Spinazzola, for his invaluable contributions to our manuscript and for supporting this project from start to finish. I also want to thank my clients, who have shown such strength and resiliency, and who are my greatest teachers.

Elizabeth Hopper

Foreword

Yoga has been practiced in the East for thousands of years, and its adepts have claimed numerous benefits: physical, emotional, and spiritual. Until recently, however, these effects have not been quantified scientifically. With Bessel A. van der Kolk's compelling research on the efficacy and positive physiological effects of yoga in trauma recovery, a vital new application for this ageless health-promoting method has been revealed. This should be of no surprise when we realize that a common denominator of all traumas is an alienation and disconnection from the body and a reduced capacity to be present in the here and now. Indeed, some survivors of trauma are attracted to yoga classes. However, many more would be overwhelmed by a room full of other people deep-breathing, sweating, chanting, and straining into seemingly impossible body postures.

In this landmark book the authors bridge this gap and offer survivors a gentle, step-by-step, *mindful* yoga that is tailored for their specific needs. They help survivors to develop a trauma-sensitive yoga practice that they can apply in the safety of their own homes. *Overcoming Trauma through Yoga* begins with a clear, accurate, and informative summary of what trauma is. It dispels common myths about trauma and invites understanding and self-compassion. The authors then help the reader to encourage present-moment experience, to learn about making choices from inner impulses, to move rhythmically within themselves, and to interact positively with others.

The next phase of the book encourages therapists to practice yoga themselves and then helps these clinicians integrate yoga-based practices into their therapy practice.

Finally, there is an informative section for yoga instructors to help them design trauma-sensitive yoga classes. The authors discuss how teachers can create a safe environment through the use of invitational, exploratory, and accepting language to promote inner experiencing. Further, they describe the qualities teachers need to cultivate in order to work effectively with traumatized students. They also give valuable advice on what to do if students are triggered in their traumatic reactions by different yoga postures and breathing patterns. In this way the risks of retraumatization are greatly reduced while healing possibilities are enhanced.

David Emerson and Elizabeth Hopper do all of this from the joined perspective of an expert yoga teacher and an experienced trauma therapist. This well-conceived book is a tremendous resource for therapists and yoga teachers. By engaging the wisdom of their bodies, it is a great companion and guide to those taking the journey of recovery from trauma to wholeness. *Overcoming Trauma through Yoga* is a gift for those taking the hero's journey of recovery and vibrancy.

Peter A. Levine, PhD, author of Waking the Tiger: Healing Trauma and In an Unspoken Voice: How the Body Releases Trauma and Restores Goodness

Foreword

When I was in graduate school, a mentor of mine said something that seemed exceedingly important. He was talking about psychoanalysis, but I thought what he said applied to all of life. He said, "The goal of psychoanalysis is to help the patient acknowledge, experience, and bear reality."

Acknowledge, experience, and bear reality. Yes! Each of those three words seemed exactly right. But I was most interested, at the time, in the final word: "bear." He was giving voice to something I already knew: the reality of our experience here on this planet can be difficult to bear.

I had never heard anyone say this quite so directly. And it came as a kind of relief to me, quite frankly, to know that others also have difficulty bearing life.

Human beings are tender creatures. We are born with our hearts open. And sometimes our open hearts encounter experiences that shatter us. Sometimes we encounter experiences that so violate our sense of safety, order, predictability, and right, that we feel utterly overwhelmed—unable to integrate, and simply unable to go on as before. Unable to bear reality. We have come to call these shattering experiences trauma. None of us is immune to them.

Trauma may result from overwhelming or violent physical experiences, or from difficult psychological and emotional experiences. Its impact may be sudden and dramatic—or the result of gradual and unrelenting violations of our very sense of self. Sometimes, we are not even aware that we're experiencing trauma until weeks, months, or even years have passed. Its damage can be quiet, creeping, and insidious.

I spent my entire childhood in a family whose life was profoundly colored by the effects of trauma—and yet we were only vaguely aware of its presence. My father—like so many of my friends' fathers—had fought in World War II. Fresh out of college and at the tender age of twenty-two—a brilliant scholar, kind, sensitive, handsome, winning—he found himself on the killing fields in Italy and Sicily with altogether too little preparation. And he was quietly tortured for the rest of his life by his experiences there.

My brother and sisters and I only recognized the poisonous effects of trauma with hindsight. All we knew as kids was that whenever a war movie came onto the TV set, Dad would quietly get up and leave the room. We would find him on the back porch smoking a cigarette and gazing into the middle distance. We found out later that his actions during the war were heroic. But he never talked about them. He could not. He simply did not have words. They had shattered something inside, very close to his heart. His quiet suffering affected us all. And perhaps the most difficult aspect of our experience as a family was that our collective trauma was never named. It was never addressed. It was invisible.

We are fortunate today to live in a time when this form of suffering is named. Over the past twenty-five years a whole cadre of experts—psychologists, social workers, doctors, nurses, neuroscientists, social scientists—have begun to drill down into the suffering of trauma, attempting, at last, to understand precisely how it works. And how it might be healed.

Our decades of study have yielded tremendous results. And one of the most interesting of these is our growing understanding of how trauma affects the body. We now recognize that trauma plays out its debilitating course *in the body.*

In trauma, the body's alarm systems turn on and then never quite turn off. And we experience the intense suffering of never truly feeling relaxed, at ease in life, always intensely on guard, with the primitive brain constantly scanning for threat or opportunity. Our inner sentry is always on watch. We cannot sleep. Our trust in the rightness of things is destroyed. Worst of all, for those of us who have been traumatized, the body becomes a kind of alien force. We perceive it as unknown, unpredictable, unreliable, even "the enemy."

But our understanding of the body's response to trauma has brought encouraging news. It is possible to intervene directly in the body's difficult state of hyperarousal. We now know that we can intentionally and systematically intervene in the body's own alarm systems and begin to turn them down.

I have seen various kinds of body interventions work dramatically—but none more so than the physical practices of yoga. Yoga is part of an ancient system meant precisely to address human suffering—and particularly to address it in the body, where it lives.

I have spent most of my adult life studying yoga. And I have come to see that it can be a particularly healing intervention for those tormented by the unhealed effects of trauma.

Yogis discovered that there are two primary roots to physical suffering. One is craving and its many effects: greed, grasping, clinging, addiction. The other is aversion: fear, terror, hatred, avoidance, anger, resentment. Trauma is an aversive state par excellence—a hardwired, persistent aversive state. Yogis—practicing intensively over the course of hundreds of years—learned to reach in and turn off the switches that control fear, terror, aversion. To turn down the volume on hatred and resentment. And to systematically begin to reestablish feelings of well-being.

Over the past ten years some of America's leading trauma experts have begun to employ yoga in the treatment of trauma. The Kripalu Institute for Extraordinary Living, which I direct, is now involved in some of the first sophisticated research into the effects of yoga on trauma.

And we are lucky now to have an excellent book exploring this emerging field. David Emerson and Elizabeth Hopper have brought us a practical and comprehensive look at the many ways in which yoga techniques can intervene in the complex processes of trauma. Their book is a clearheaded and compelling investigation of yoga and trauma. It will offer a very practical form of hope to thousands, and a platform for the development of a new wing of trauma research. It is a welcome and important contribution, and I recommend it to you.

Stephen Cope, MSW, director of the Kripalu Institute for Extraordinary Living and author of *Yoga and the Quest for the True Self*

Introduction

BESSEL A. VAN DER KOLK, MD

*Founder and Medical Director of the
Trauma Center at Justice Resource Institute*

There must be many different things that inspire people to develop a yoga practice, and what got us at the Trauma Center involved in yoga was rather peculiar. After all, what does it take to get a rather conventional person to stand on one leg with his fingers pointing at the sky for prolonged periods of time, or to casually lie on the floor to assume the posture of a happy baby?

Somewhere around 1999 we became familiar with a new biological marker called heart rate variability (HRV). HRV had recently been discovered to be a good way to measure the integrity of one of the brain's arousal systems, the one located in the oldest part of the brain: the brain stem. Well-regulated people tend to have robust HRV, which is reflected in their ability to have a reasonable degree of control over their impulses and emotions. This is mirrored in the capacity of their inhalations and exhalations to produce rhythmical fluctuations in heart rate. People who are easily thrown off balance tend to have low HRV, and they also are at risk for developing a variety of illnesses, including depression, heart disease, and cancer.

After several months we had collected enough tracings of our traumatized patients to make us conclude that they have unusually low HRV. This could help explain why traumatized people are so reactive to minor stresses and so prone to develop a variety of physical illnesses. Aside from our scientific interest, there also was a more personal one. While we were experimenting with HRV, we measured the integrity of our own brain stem regulatory systems, as well, and discovered that my own HRV was not nearly robust enough to guarantee long-term physical health. Thus, we had a double incentive to start concentrating on improving HRV, both to protect our patients against losing their cool and getting sick, and to find a way of taking care of my own recently diagnosed brain stem dysregulation.

We looked on the internet to see what research had shown to help improve HRV. Google listed 17,000 yoga sites that claimed that yoga changes HRV, but when I looked up what studies had been done to prove that this is, in fact, true, the search engine produced no results. Yogis may have developed a wonderful method to help people find an internal balance, but there is not much of a scientific tradition of measuring the various claims of what yoga can and cannot do.

A few days after we started to think about ways in which we could improve people's HRV, David Emerson walked through the front door of the Trauma Center. He introduced himself as a yoga teacher who had been working with war veterans at a local vet center and developing a modified form of hatha yoga to help these trauma survivors. Dave asked us if we would be interested in collaborating to study the efficacy of yoga as a treatment for PTSD. We looked around for a space to teach yoga classes and figured out how we should formally measure how yoga affects PTSD. This collaboration led to one of the most gratifying programs at the Trauma Center. Yoga became a major cornerstone in our understanding that it is imperative to befriend one's bodily sensations to overcome the imprints of trauma.

Why did yoga provide a key to recovery from traumatic stress? Our work with traumatized children and adults had taught us that assaults can cause a disintegration of people's self-protective capacities. Our bodies are programmed to automatically respond to physical threats by fighting or fleeing. An experience becomes traumatic when this natural flight/flight defense is aborted. When you are assaulted and realize that there is nothing you can do to stave off the inevitable, this self-protective system may break down, resulting in the inappropriate activation of fight/flight reactions in response to minor subsequent irritations, and an inability to regain a sense of safety and relaxation.

While the mind usually shuts down during a traumatizing experience, the bodily sensations associated with immobilization and helplessness carry the memories of having absolutely no control over the outcome of your life: the fate of trauma survivors is lived out in heartbreak and gut-wrenching sensations.

The most profound legacy of trauma may be this timeless feeling of being battered by unbearable physical sensations: crushing feelings in your chest, agonizing tension in your shoulders, and burning pain in your abdomen, accompanied by the conviction that you are utterly helpless to do anything about it. The body, instead of being an ally on one's road to recovery, becomes the enemy. Many traumatized people learn to tell a story of what happened, so that friends and relatives can understand why they are so frightened, angry, or out of control, but the real problem is that they do not feel safe inside—their own bodies have become booby-trapped. As a result, it is not OK to feel what you feel and know what you know, because your body has become the container of dread and horror. The enemy who started on the outside is transformed into an inner torment.

Our own developing yoga program, which initially focused on studying whether yoga could, indeed, change HRV (and we found that it does), gradually helped us realize that yoga could provide one way to help traumatized people relearn to inhabit their tortured bodies. My patient Anna had been dreadfully sexually abused by both her father and her mother between the time she was three and seven years old. Even as an adult she coped with the memories of her abuse by making her mind disappear whenever she had to deal with disagreements and confrontations. When she felt overwhelmed, she found relief by taking a razor blade and making deep cuts into her body. After years of various forms of therapy, she consulted me, and I suggested that she might be able to achieve a more loving relationship with her body by joining our yoga program. After the first two classes she wrote to me:

> I don't know all of the reasons that yoga terrifies me so much, but I do know that it will be an incredible source of healing for me, and that is why I am working on myself to try it. Yoga is about looking inward instead of outward and listening to my body, and a lot of my survival has been geared around never doing those things. Going to the class today, my heart was racing, and part of me really wanted to turn around, but then I just kept putting one foot in front of the other until I got to the door and went in. After the class I came home and slept for four hours. This week I was doing yoga at home, and the words

came to me, "Your body has things to say."
I said back to myself, "I will try and listen."

Anna comes to my office once a week for therapy, but in between she likes to stay in touch and regularly emails me about what is going on with her. After about a month of doing yoga Anna wrote to me again:

> I talked to David a little bit about how I push myself to breathe to those parts of my body that have been tortured, when I naturally stop my breath from going there. Today when I was doing yoga, I tried to just send the breath to my trunk on both sides when I was in positions that are supposed to help open up the hips. I could feel how tight I was there, and some part of me told my body I was sorry for letting it hold all that stuff alone. Then all of a sudden I felt like I was inside of my body and I could feel myself being abused by my father, but from the inside, not from the outside. I started to see it happening. I didn't feel pain, and I didn't feel too scared, but I noticed exactly what was happening, and some part of me accepted it as in "Yes, that happened." Am I making any sense to you? In a strange way, this felt like movement forward, not backward. This yoga stuff is mind-blowing.

When people deal with trauma in conventional psychotherapy, they usually focus primarily on telling what has happened in the past. Discussions typically are concerned with how being reminded of old terror can trigger fear, rage, or paralysis in the present. Many people experience relief being able to discuss how seeing certain images, hearing particular sounds, or smelling a specific odor causes them to feel as if the trauma were happening right now. However, reliving trauma-related sensations does not occur only in response to input from our surroundings; it also is triggered by sensations deep within our own bodies: the sensory experiences that are evoked by feeling angry, sexually aroused, or having your period; by feeling tender toward somebody; or by the sensations that accompany feeling rejected and underappreciated.

Maybe the most difficult part of having been traumatized is dealing with the triggers that reside inside. The trauma is a thing of the past, but your body keeps reacting as if you still are in imminent danger. These internal triggers transform your inner world into a minefield. At least the trauma itself had a beginning, middle, and end, but these triggers may come at any time, like a thief in the night, at the most inopportune moments. You know that you should not feel this way, but your body keeps getting hijacked into feeling intolerable sensations and emotions. This makes you feel crazy: on some level you realize that the danger is over, but your insides, the sensations that churn around in your body, keep warning you of impending doom. Trapped once again, you respond with terror, rage, and helplessness.

The problem is not only what happens inside our minds or even our bodies—trauma affects the totality of our organism. As the late body psychotherapist Thomas Hanna said in *The Body of Life,*

> We cannot hate or be angry without an organism that hates and is angry. We cannot love and hope and expect without actively, movingly, physiologically loving and hoping and expecting. Hate, anger, love, and hope are not "psychological states," existing in some "mental" vacuum; they are somatic states that exist in the entirety of a living organism.

Most people I see in my practice have become experts in bracing against their inner sensations and in ignoring the inner world of their bodies. The lives of many trauma survivors come to revolve around isolating and neutralizing unwanted sensory experiences—at least half of the traumatized people I have treated have tried to dull their intolerable inner world with drugs or alcohol. Many traumatized people learn that self-injury such as cutting can make these sensations go away. Others race motorcycles or engage in other high-risk activities, like prostitution or gambling, which they say gives them a sense of control or provides relief by giving them an emotional "high."

Injured people involuntary find a way to physically protect themselves against the unbidden messages of danger and dissolution that continue to emanate from their bodies. They brace themselves against unacceptable physical sensations. People who are scared all the time develop bodies that somehow protect against this anxiety. There is a multiplicity of ways of doing that, and many trauma survivors unconsciously try out several different ones over time. Preoccupied with losing control, they stiffen their muscles, which prevents them from relaxing and being able to go with the flow. Their tension ultimately may lead to muscle spasms, migraine headaches, fibromyalgia, and chronic pain. Once these conditions are medicalized, they develop a life of their own, leading to regular doctor visits, diagnostic tests, medications, and rehabilitation programs, none of which is likely to address the underlying issues.

A person whose fundamental preoccupation is to be ready for the next assault is also likely to generate a constant torrent of thoughts related to survival. This may range from obsessive rage against real and imaginary assailants to relentless worrying about having provoked rejection and abandonment. Such thoughts automatically reinforce the feedback loop with the body's physiology and immune systems, which are stimulated into staying in unrelenting attack or defense modes. The constant repetition of vengeful thoughts will relentlessly activate the same muscles and glands of our bodies, just as preoccupation with defeat and disappointment will become imprinted into our bodily tissues until they droop in despondency. Constant preoccupation with our injuries, misery, resentments, or dread is in itself a self-injurious activity.

When children grow up unheard or not seen, and thus do not have their physiological states mirrored by the people they depend on for nurturance and regulation—or when adults are constantly triggered by unbearable physical sensations—they become separated from the vital connection to their bodies. The childhood imprints of who you are, and who the people you interact with are, continue to unconsciously guide interactions with others well into adulthood. Recurrent activation of schemas of abandonment and assault cause confusion about the reality of our lives and form the basis of our day-to-day suffering. This prevents us from living life to its fullest. The ability to receive, process, and enjoy or tolerate pleasure and pain becomes impaired.

People who have never been safely and securely held lack the visceral experience of a calmly abiding center: a deep sense of being absolutely all right and absolutely safe. This was reflected in our research on yoga with chronically traumatized women: we observed that during Savasana, the state of total relaxation at the end of a yoga session, their muscles continued to twitch, as if still fighting an unseen enemy. We saw this also in our immunology research, where the immune systems of incest victims were shown to be excessively activated, as if they were in acute danger of being assaulted by environmental toxins. Our research suggested that this excessive alertness to danger could predispose these women to develop autoimmune illnesses.

One of the profound lessons from contemporary neuroscience research is that our sense of ourselves is anchored in a vital connection with our bodies. The neuroscientist Antonio Damasio has shown that an area of the brain called the insula is the place that transmits bodily sensations into conscious awareness. This means that consciousness is fundamentally a product of how we interpret the physical sensations that we experience. Brain imaging studies of traumatized people repeatedly show decreased activation in the insula and other areas related to self-awareness.

Most forms of traditional psychotherapy focus on the interplay between emotions and thought, as in, "So how do you feel about that?" in response to somebody recounting an event, or, "Let's reflect on that, and see how we can make sense of it" when somebody is upset about something that has happened. When a person is distressed, standard therapy tries to figure out what makes something so disturbing, and what you can do to change it. Most thera-pies downplay or ignore the shifts in people's inner sensory world that carry the essence of the organisms' responses: the emotional states that are imprinted in the state of the body's chemical profile, the state of one's viscera, and the contraction of the striated muscles of the face, throat, trunk, and limbs. Yet, that is the level on which the trauma continues to be played out—in the theater of the body. That being the case, people who are traumatized need to have physical and sensory experiences to unlock their bodies, activate effective fight/flight responses, tolerate their sensations, befriend their inner experiences, and cultivate new action patterns.

My friend Diana Fosha has pointed out that being able to tolerate visceral experience is indispensable in being able to change one's fundamental approach to life. Hence, change depends on the capacity to experience emotions directly and deeply. If our access to core experience is blocked or distorted, we are unable to deal with our most vital psychological processes.

Learning to tolerate and be curious about dreaded physical sensations gives people a sense of mastery. The visceral experience of mastery, involving emotions and sensations, provides new resources, energy, and the capacity to take effective action. Somatic experiencing, with an intuitive knowledge that there is a natural flow in and out of emotions, opens up an appetite for even deeper experiencing.

Anna gradually learned to tolerate horrible memories without becoming overwhelmed. In the first two years of therapy, overwhelming emotions of fear, shame, and humiliation would cause Anna to shut down and become speechless—she would cover her eyes with her hands, and her legs would shake uncontrollably. Now she can notice, be curious, and observe.

Yoga is part of the overall healing process. Being able to find the words that allow you to know what happened, and being able to place the memory in space and time, liberates a person from the tyranny of having to relive the trauma in the present. But only if the past can be remembered without the body being forced to relive what happened can one truly speak of recovery.

one

Reclaiming Your Body

The goal of treatment of PTSD [post-traumatic stress disorder] is to help people live in the present, without feeling or behaving according to irrelevant demands belonging to the past.

BESSEL A. VAN DER KOLK[1]

Trauma has touched most of our lives in one way or another. Trauma takes many forms: from abuse at home to sexual assault, experience in war, and many other difficult experiences. Some of us have experienced accidents, disasters, interpersonal violence and abuse, medical trauma, or traumatic losses, while others of us have been exposed to trauma indirectly through the experiences of friends or loved ones.

In some cases, trauma overwhelms our ability to cope, and the resulting symptoms can be debilitating. We may have trouble falling asleep or wake up from nightmares. We may be bothered by recurrent memories of the trauma and have to work hard to avoid those thoughts. We may struggle with negative thoughts about ourselves or have difficulties in our relationships.

This book is for people who have experienced the devastating effects of trauma and for the teachers and providers who work with them. It is intended to offer some direct, action-oriented practices that survivors can use as they see fit. We will present many exercises throughout the book, and readers are welcome to experiment with any of these that seem interesting; in that way, this book is a practice manual. We also wish to share some information with caregivers, namely therapists and yoga instructors, to increase their confidence in offering trauma-informed yoga practices as part of the healing process. Our hope is that readers will feel comfortable using the practices themselves and sharing the material with supportive people in their lives with whom they may safely explore some of these exercises.

Because of the prevalence of trauma in our society, many of us face multiple threats to our physical and emotional safety throughout our lives. Consider for a moment the following statistics. According to a national incidence study of abuse and neglect, nearly three million children—one out of every twenty-five children—experience some form of endangerment each year in the United States, and almost a third of these children experience direct physical, sexual, or emotional abuse. In any given year, more than two million children experience significant physical or emotional neglect.[2] Recent findings have indicated that emotional neglect can be as detrimental to a child as physical or sexual abuse.[3] By the time a child reaches the age of eighteen, the probability that he or she will have been directly affected by interpersonal or community violence is approximately one in four.[4]

Many of these children will experience immediate consequences, such as difficulty sleeping, problems concentrating in school, difficulty calming down, and troubled peer relationships. However, the full impact of childhood trauma more often does not manifest itself until years later, in adolescence and adulthood.[5] As a consequence, adults often mistakenly assume that a child who has been exposed to trauma has escaped unscathed because he or she does not initially exhibit overt symptoms of distress or impairment.

Interpersonal violence and abuse are also rampant in adulthood. According to the National Institute of Justice and the Centers for Disease Control, nearly one-fifth of women, and one in thirty-three men, report experiencing a completed or attempted rape at some time in their lives. Each year in the United States, approximately 1.3 million women and 835,000 men are physically assaulted by an intimate partner.[6] The surgeon general's office has reported that domestic violence is the leading cause of injury to women between the ages of fifteen and forty-four, making it more common than automobile accidents, muggings, and cancer deaths combined.

In addition to interpersonal violence, trauma can also take the form of accidents, war, illness and medical intervention, the death of loved ones, natural disasters, and many other types of events. People can also experience "vicarious trauma" reactions from hearing about or seeing traumatic events, or from being aware of loved ones' suffering as a result of exposure to traumatic events.

The common denominator of all of these traumatic experiences is that they involve some sort of threat to our physical, emotional, and/or psychological safety. Describing the impact of trauma is difficult because it is so dependent on the individual's subjective experience. In their recent book *Treating Traumatic Stress in Children and Adolescents*, authors Blaustein and Kinniburgh note,

> The experience of trauma is complex. Trauma varies in type, source, chronicity, and impact; it is experienced at different developmental stages, within different contexts—family, community, and culture—and in the presence or absence of different internal and external resources and challenges. It is not surprising, then, that disparity exists in our understanding of trauma, its manifestations, and its proper treatment.[7]

We do know that, for many people, exposure to trauma has a profound impact on health and well-being. In the United States alone, around 7.7 million American adults age eighteen and older, or about 3.5 percent of adults in a given year, suffer from post-traumatic stress disorder (PTSD).[8] Researchers have begun to describe impacts on the traumatized brain and are recognizing some very important neurophysiological and neuroanatomical differences between the brains of people who are suffering from PTSD or other trauma-related symptoms and those who are not. For instance, there are structural differences in the brains of individuals with PTSD, such as decreased hippocampal volume in adulthood and differences in multiple frontal-limbic structures.[9]

Many of the trauma survivors that we work with experience PTSD as merely the tip of the iceberg, and not uncommonly, this diagnosis is not present at all. For individuals who have endured years of exposure to traumatic events, particularly childhood maltreatment or neglect or subsequent prolonged relationship violence, the cost of survival often includes a far more complex array of medical and psychiatric conditions and impediments to learning, productive social and occupational functioning, and physical health and well-being.[10]

The Adverse Childhood Experiences (ACE) study is a major research study that links adult health status to child abuse (psychological, physical, or sexual) and household dysfunction experienced during childhood (exposure to domestic violence, or living with household members who abused drugs or alcohol, were mentally ill or suicidal, or had engaged in criminal behavior). These studies found that childhood trauma has a cumulative effect and is associated with a much higher risk of developing serious substance abuse or dependence, depression, and suicidality in adulthood. The cumulative effects of childhood trauma are also related to a higher risk of a number of the leading causes of death in adults, including obesity, ischemic heart disease, cancer, chronic lung disease, skeletal fractures, and liver disease.[11]

Measurable effects of trauma have been well documented in the literature. In this book, we will move beyond this objective focus to an emphasis on the subjective experience of trauma as felt in the body. For many people, trauma is a process of very literally losing control of their body. When a traumatic event occurs, our bodies rally to get us away from the danger: our heart rate increases; our muscles tense; we increase our oxygen intake through more rapid breathing; and our brain diverts energy away from language and meaning-making centers to sensory awareness, muscle enervation, and emotional responses. These processes are designed to help us fight off or escape an attack.

Some clinicians speculate that PTSD occurs when all of these natural, physiological processes are rendered ineffectual—when we are overpowered and held down by the attacker; when the car crashes into us and we are trapped in the middle of the destruction; when, in childhood, we are living in fear and confusion, never knowing when the grown-up upon whose love and protection we are dependent is going to hurt us next—above all, when the trauma persists despite our best efforts to escape it. The survival system is working, but the final link in the chain is not made: we cannot move; we are stuck. The traumatic event occurs despite the fact that everything we are—our physical, intellectual, emotional, and neurobiological selves—is trying to help us get away. When this occurs, we can become deeply wounded, left with the sense that our own body has betrayed us by failing to get us to safety. As trauma expert Judith Herman puts it, survivors come to "feel unsafe in their bodies."[12]

As a result of this perceived betrayal, we are left with some very difficult, if sometimes unconscious, choices. For example, how can we nourish and care for this body that has been the cause of so much pain? Our relationship to our own body is often one great casualty of trauma. We may give up on taking care of ourselves on many levels, which can manifest in drug and alcohol abuse, high-risk sexual behaviors, extreme weight loss or obesity, or self-harming behavior. These ways of living with our body cause further harm and may ultimately become unsustainable. We need to find other ways of coping with the pain that we experience when we are aware of ourselves and our bodies.

Clinicians have begun to recognize that "traditional psychotherapy addresses the cognitive and emotional elements of trauma, but lacks techniques that work directly with the physiological elements, despite the fact that trauma profoundly affects the body and many symptoms of traumatized individuals are somatically based."[13] Those of us involved in helping trauma survivors need to broaden our methodology beyond talk therapy and bring the body into the healing milieu. While talk-based therapy serves a critical role in the healing process, many are finding that it is insufficient by itself. We must address the ways that trauma is held in the body in order to make the healing process more complete.

At the Trauma Center at Justice Resource Institute (JRI), a world-renowned center for the research and treatment of trauma, we have introduced trauma-sensitive yoga as an adjunctive treatment for trauma survivors. We view trauma-sensitive yoga as a way to make peace with your body, to learn through experience that your body can be effective again, and to reclaim your body as your own. We also believe that the lessons learned through trauma-sensitive yoga can translate into a more generalized acceptance of, and trust in, one's own self.

Our approach to yoga at the Trauma Center is unique because it is trauma-informed; this is why we call it *trauma-sensitive yoga.* Everything we do takes place in a clinical milieu, is directly informed by our own unique research, and is developed in collaboration between yoga teachers and clinicians who have expertise in trauma-related issues. Since 2006, we have trained hundreds of health care professionals and yoga teachers from all over the world who work with trauma survivors and use our principles and practice of traumasensitive yoga. There is a growing movement of trauma-informed clinicians offering yoga-based interventions within the context of individual therapy, as well as yoga-based groups or classes within therapeutic milieus, such as residential treatment programs or outpatient treatment centers.

This book tells the story of how trauma-sensitive yoga is emerging as an effective adjunctive treatment for trauma survivors. For clinicians and yoga teachers, we want to provide you with a framework for considering body-based interventions and will share some of our experiences in modifying yoga to meet the needs of survivors of trauma. For survivors, we hope to give you a context for understanding your own reactions, a rationale for the use of yoga as a healing practice, and some specific practices that you can incorporate into your own path toward healing.

A Welcome Practice

As we move through the book, we will address many issues that are important in a trauma-sensitive yoga practice. We will come back to an explanation of the language that we use, accommodations that we make, choices that are offered, and so on. However, because this is a book about taking effective action, let's begin with an exercise.

If you like, take a moment to find a comfortable seat. You may choose to sit in a chair or on the floor. You may decide to use pillows to prop yourself up in a comfortable way. If you are lying in bed due to a medical or physical condition, your bed will serve as your "seat." In any case, give yourself a moment to adjust so that you are reasonably at ease where you are. Feel free to move and adjust in order to make yourself more comfortable. Your movements may be very small, or they may be bigger. If you like, notice how you are moving and adjusting as you consider making yourself more comfortable.

When you are ready, take a moment to notice where you are connected to the floor. If you are sitting in a chair, it may be your feet that are on the ground. If you are lying in bed, you may notice that you are connected to the floor through the structure of the bed. If you are sitting on the floor, notice what part of your body is connected to the floor. If you like, give yourself a moment to notice, as best you can, where and how you are connected to the floor beneath you.

Finally, if you like, as a practice, feel free to interact with how you are connected to the floor. You can move your body, wiggle your toes, or shift your weight around as a way of bringing attention to your connection to the floor beneath you.

Again, as you do this practice of interacting with how you are connected to the floor beneath you, just notice what you notice. It may be flickers of sensation—brief moments of connection. If you like, focus on those moments and investigate them for a few breaths. (Using breath is one way to track duration in these yoga practices. You may wish to take one to three breaths as you investigate each aspect of a practice.)

When you are ready, feel free to let this practice go and move on.

two

Traumatic Stress

A Brief History of Traumatic Stress and Trauma Treatment

Traumatic experiences have existed throughout history; however, our understanding of the meaning of these experiences and their impact on people has changed dramatically over time. We would like to offer a brief historical perspective on the progress that has been made in our understanding of the impact of traumatic stress, and on interventions that have been used to address traumatic stress symptoms.

Historical Views on Mental Health Symptoms

In ancient Greece, Hippocrates, the father of modern Western medicine, proposed a connection between the body's physiology and mental and emotional states. He believed that health was based on a balance among four "humors," or fluids, in the body. Although his theories were primarily reductionist, linking emotions directly to physiological explanations, he did make links between traumatic losses and subsequent symptoms in some of his writings. For instance, he described one woman who experienced fears, depression, and incoherent speech and another who, "without speaking a word ... would fumble, pluck, scratch, pick hairs, weep and then laugh, but ... not speak"; both of these women were responding to some sort of "grief."[1] Around five hundred years later, another Greek physician, Galen, distinguished between symptoms that were caused by organic, or physical, causes and those that looked similar but resulted from purely emotional causes.[2]

One of the earliest labels for mental health symptoms, or symptoms with no apparent physical basis, was *hysteria*. This term was used from the seventeenth through the nineteenth centuries to describe numerous symptoms in women, including nervousness, irritability, insomnia, shortness of breath, loss of appetite, and a loss of sexual interest. The term stems from the Greek word for uterus, *hystera*, and emerged from an ancient Greek myth about the uterus wandering through the body, causing dysfunction. Hysteria incorporated symptoms from what is currently a broad range of disorders described in the American Psychiatric Association's *Diagnostic and Statistical Manual of Mental Disorders* (DSM), including posttraumatic stress disorder (PTSD), anxiety disorders, mood disorders, dissociative disorders, and somatization disorders. Hysteria remained a primary explanation for mental health symptoms in women for over two centuries, but conceptualizations of what was meant by "hysteria" varied widely.[3] This gender-biased conceptualization of mental illness has subsequently been refuted by scholars as reflecting the historical and political context at that time, which emerged from patriarchal ideologies.

Link between Traumatic Events and Symptoms

In the mid-1800s, physician John Eric Erichsen made the link between traumatic events and symptoms that have no physical basis. With the advent of railroad transportation around this time, railway workers suffered numerous accidents, injuries, and deaths. Erichsen described a constellation of symptoms, which he termed "railway spine," that included headaches, dizziness, paralysis, general disinterest, listlessness, memory loss, confusion, diminished business aptitude, ill temper, sleep disorders, sensory impairment, attitude changes, loss of motor power, numbness, and sexual impotence.[4] While some of these symptoms may have been due to head injuries, other cases might have reflected what is currently understood as post-traumatic stress.

Jean-Martin Charcot (1825–1893), known as the father of modern neurology, researched hysteria to identify common patterns among symptoms.[5] He established a clear connection between a traumatic stimulus and the symptoms seen in "hysteria." He suggested that individuals had an inherited, constitutional vulnerability toward the development of hysteria, but that the illness was often triggered by a traumatic event. Charcot utilized hypnosis to induce a state of hysteria in patients in order to study the phenomenon, and he also introduced hypnosis as a treatment for hysteria.[6]

Sigmund Freud (1856–1939), a student of Charcot, founded the psychoanalytic school of psychiatry. The treatment of trauma in the first half of the twentieth century often involved psychoanalysis, an intervention in which the therapist acts as a "blank slate," allowing elements of the patient's unconscious to emerge. Patients were assumed to use "defense mechanisms" to protect against elements of their unconscious. Freud's approach to the issue of trauma varied throughout the course of his work. Freud's initial theory was that neurosis had its origins in trauma, termed *traumatic neurosis*. After working with numerous female clients who reported childhood sexual abuse, he initially considered a "passive sexual experience before puberty" to be the "specific aetiology [cause] of hysteria."[7] He began to develop techniques such as interpreting symbols to elicit "scenes" of sexual abuse from many of his patients. Freud believed that these scenes represented repressed, unconscious memories. Along with his colleague physician Josef Breuer, Freud emphasized abreaction,[8] which involved verbal expression along with emotional discharge, as a treatment.[9] Later in life, Freud rejected his early theories in favor of developmental models, but he still believed that responses to actual trauma could be differentiated from symptoms that were the product of developmental fixation.

Pierre Janet (1859–1947) explored and described the role of dissociation in traumatic hysteria.[10] Janet asserted that intense emotions interfere with appraisal of and appropriate responses to an event, leading to dissociation of traumatic memories. These unacknowledged memories then intrude as sensory experiences (visual images, auditory memories, tactile sensations), overwhelming emotions, and behaviors that repeat elements of the original trauma (behavioral reenactments). Contemporary traumatic stress experts view Janet as central to the development of this field: "a century later, Janet still provides an unsurpassed framework for integrating current knowledge about the psychodynamic, cognitive, and biological effects of human traumatization."[11] Janet's work was a predecessor of current-day phase-oriented trauma intervention models. His framework reflected three stages of treatment highlighted by these models: "(1) stabilization and symptom reduction, (2) identification and modification of traumatic memories, and (3) reintegration and rehabilitation."[12]

Veterans and Traumatic Stress

World War I brought increasing attention to trauma-related symptoms when a wave of soldiers returned home with a host of unexplained symptoms. Many men who had been exposed to extreme violence suffered from motoric symptoms such as shakes, stutters, tics, tremors, and gait problems, leaving them incapacitated. They also reported sensory problems, such as vision and hearing impairment, that did not appear to have any physical basis.[13] Freud's ideas about the unconscious emotional origins of hysterical symptoms were applied to these veterans and were interpreted as a conflict between fear and duty resulting in a "flight into illness." The experiences of these soldiers, many of whom were considered to have "conversion hysteria," demonstrated that the impact of traumatic stress crosses gender lines. Abram Kardiner, an American physician and analyst, described the physioneurosis in traumatic war neurosis as a defense that was intended to ward off the trauma, but which led to adaptive failure.[14] A number of new terms for trauma-related illness were introduced around this time, including "shell fever," "mental shock," "war shock," "shell shock," and "war psychoneurosis." World War II supplied further confirmation of a trauma-related syndrome in combat veterans. "Battle fatigue" and "combat exhaustion" were new terms that emerged around this time.

After the Second World War, the American Psychiatric Association developed its initial *Diagnostic and Statistical Manual of Mental Disorders*. The DSM described the symptoms commonly seen in war veterans as *gross stress reaction*. Gross stress reaction described acute psychological responses following exposure to an extreme stressor that would be traumatic for most people and that resolved after the stressor ceased. There was no mention of longer-lasting symptoms following exposure to a traumatic stressor. Around this time, posttrauma reactions were also discovered among Holocaust survivors, prisoners-of-war, and the survivors of mass catastrophes. Despite the clarification of these post-trauma responses, the second edition of the DSM, published in 1968, excluded any diagnostic categories for trauma-related symptoms.[15]

Following the Vietnam War, veterans, members of the public, and professionals advocated for the inclusion of a trauma-related syndrome in the next revision of the DSM. In response, when published in 1980, DSM-III included the term commonly used today to describe trauma-related illness, post-traumatic stress disorder (PTSD).[16]

Expansion of the Application of the PTSD Diagnosis

In the past three decades, the concept of post-traumatic stress disorder has become widely accepted. In the 1980s, the term expanded from a narrower focus on war-related trauma to include the aftereffects of domestic violence, sexual assault, and child abuse. Dissociative processes also received increased consideration in DSM-III, with elaboration and grouping of five Dissociative Disorders as an independent diagnostic category, despite their close association to traumatic stress.[17]

In the 1980s and 1990s, researchers began to make links between the body's normal survival response and the symptoms commonly seen in PTSD, clarifying the physiological basis of the PTSD response. This understanding led to an increase in the number of treatments available for trauma-related syndromes.

Modern-Day Treatment Models for Post-traumatic Stress

Treatment models during the 1970s and 1980s emphasized the importance of catharsis, a treatment that involved "letting out" all of the feelings and memories associated with the traumatic event. This model of treatment reflected back to Freud and Breuer's earlier emphasis on abreaction. This type of treatment was based on the assumption that avoidance of memories of traumatic exposure and associated feelings was the cause of post-traumatic stress symptoms. This model appealed to many survivors who wanted to somehow "get rid of" these memories or "clear them out."

Cognitive behavioral therapies such as exposure therapy and cognitive processing therapy have dominated contemporary treatment outcome research for PTSD. In the 1980s and 1990s, the concept of exposure therapy[18] as a treatment for trauma became popular. This type of treatment is based on behavioral models of anxiety in which the client is seen as avoiding traumatic reminders. According to these models, avoidance serves to increase the intensity of anxiety regarding the traumatic events because there are no opportunities to unlearn fear-based associations. Treatment therefore involves exposing the client to traumatic reminders. One type of exposure therapy is systematic desensitization, in which the client is gradually exposed to increasingly intense reminders of the trauma while practicing relaxation skills. Prolonged exposure therapy,[19] developed by Edna Foa, is a treatment in which clients are exposed for extended periods of time to detailed elements of their traumatic memories. The intensity of clients' anxiety and avoidance is assumed to decrease over time with the prolonged exposure.

Cognitive processing therapy (CPT), developed by Patricia Resick, combines exposure with cognitive restructuring. The goal of this type of therapy is to identify beliefs that clients are holding about themselves, others, and the world, and to help them shift schemas that are contributing to their trauma-related symptoms.[20]

In addition to cognitive behavioral therapies, a wide range of approaches have been supported for chronic traumatic stress symptoms, including group therapy, psychodynamic therapies, hypnosis, psychosocial rehabilitation, eye movement desensitization and reprocessing (EMDR; see below for a description), school-based therapy, couple and family therapy, and creative therapies. Psychopharmacological treatment of trauma-related symptoms is also common. Common medications include selective serotonin reuptake inhibitor (SSRI) antidepressants and newer antidepressants known as serotonin–norepinephrine reuptake inhibitors (SNRIs); other medications have also been used, with varying effectiveness and side effects.[21] A recent meta-analysis demonstrated that all of the trauma-focused treatments were found to be about equally effective across studies; as a whole, trauma-focused treatments were more effective than were traditional or supportive therapy approaches not focused on trauma.[22]

Complex Trauma and the Limitations of Available Treatment Models

In the last twenty years, pioneers in the field of traumatic stress, such as Bessel A. van der Kolk and Judith Herman, have challenged the limitations of the PTSD diagnosis as the sole diagnostic category available for trauma-related conditions. They found that chronic interpersonal trauma exposure, particularly during early development, often results in a more profound and wider-ranging impact than is described within a PTSD diagnosis. Individuals who have survived chronic or repeated traumas, especially those who were exposed to trauma during critical developmental periods, are affected holistically: mind, body, and spirit. Survivors of chronic or repeated abuse often experience extreme difficulty managing their own emotions and negotiating healthy and rewarding friendships and intimate relationships. They characteristically harbor persistent feelings of worthlessness and shame and grapple with intense personal scrutiny and self-blame. This negative self-appraisal tends to derive initially from survivors' perceived responsibility for the traumatic events they endured, but often it is ultimately generalized to consume the majority of their life experiences, decisions, and actions. *Complex trauma* is a term that was coined to describe these more profound sequelae associated with living in a prolonged environment of maltreatment and neglect. Complex PTSD includes the following constellation of symptoms: affect dysregulation; dissociation; somatic disturbance; negative or distorted self-image; impaired capacity to initiate, navigate, or sustain human relationships; and rupture of one's fundamental beliefs and systems of meaning.[23]

Although exposure therapy is widely considered to be an efficacious treatment for many people suffering from PTSD,[24] other people have difficulty tolerating exposure-based treatment. Exposure to traumatic memories often leads to an increase in physiological and/or emotional distress, followed by a more gradual decline in emotional intensity with habituation to the material. However, many individuals with complex trauma have not developed the internal and external resources necessary to tolerate the intensity of the physiological and emotional experiences that often emerge during exposure. Clinicians often report that they do not use exposure therapies due to concerns that their clients' symptoms may worsen, that they may drop out of treatment prematurely, or that they will have difficulty tolerating the treatment.[25]

Unfortunately, much of the treatment outcome research on trauma-related issues does not reflect the unique needs of individuals who are struggling with complex trauma. Many standardized treatment outcome studies have excluded large numbers of participants based on the severity and complexity of their symptoms, and many of these studies have also had high dropout rates among participants.[26] Because of this, the conclusions drawn from these studies may not be applicable to individuals with complex trauma. Researchers have begun to look at the individuals who worsened or who were excluded from the majority of treatment outcome studies[27] in an attempt to identify alternative treatments that would be more effective for these individuals.

More Recent Treatments

As a result of the increasing awareness of the complexity of trauma responses, experts have begun to develop alternative treatments that address the unique needs of individuals with complex trauma. These interventions typically focus on building coping skills prior to addressing traumatic memories. For instance, Marylene Cloitre developed the Skills Training in Affective and Interpersonal Regulation (STAIR) model of treatment,[28] which focuses on the development of self-regulation skills prior to creating a trauma narrative.

While not designed as a trauma-specific treatment model, dialectical behavioral therapy (DBT), an intervention developed by Marsha Linehan, focuses on the development of a number of important psychological capacities and skills (mindfulness, distress tolerance, emotional regulation, and interpersonal effectiveness) that are often lacking or severely underdeveloped in chronic trauma survivors.[29] At the Trauma Center, we have found it to be beneficial to integrate elements of DBT into the overarching trauma-focused treatment plans for many of our clients.

Eye movement desensitization and reprocessing (EMDR) is a particularly innovative and unique trauma-processing intervention that helps survivors to integrate emotional, cognitive, and somatic elements of their traumatic experiences into the larger context of their lives.[30] Although EMDR was developed as a trauma-processing therapy, more recent "Resource Identification and Installation" protocols in EMDR treatment have provided an emphasis on building resiliency prior to an exploration of traumatic memories.[31] Experts in child traumatic stress have also begun to develop intervention frameworks that address the unique needs of children with complex trauma responses, and that focus on the development of regulatory capacities and on the development of strengths and resiliency.[32]

The Future of Trauma Treatment

The cutting edge of trauma treatment today involves alternative and integrative intervention strategies that move beyond traditional verbal therapies. Bessel A. van der Kolk has asserted that "describing traumatic experiences in conventional verbal therapy is likely to activate implicit memories, that is, trauma-related physical sensations and physiological hyper-or hypoarousal, which evoke emotions such as helplessness, fear, shame, and rage. When this occurs, trauma victims are prone to feeling that it is still not safe to deal with the trauma."[33] Many newer interventions focus on the development of resources and use a "bottom-up" approach that integrates the body into treatment. For instance, sensorimotor psychotherapy[34] is a type of therapy that uses the body as an entryway to exploring a client's resources and unprocessed traumatic memories. Newly emerging creative therapies—including application of art, dance, music, and theater-based approaches to intervention—focus on the integration of the mind and body for healing. Similarly, the practice of yoga offers a platform for body-based intervention with trauma survivors. Yoga-based interventions assimilate physical movement and restorative action patterns into treatment, and in doing so they endeavor to help trauma survivors build internal strengths and resources in an embodied manner. Along with similar body-based strategies, yoga is at the frontier of trauma treatment in promoting mind/body healing.

Trauma and the Survival Response

The fact that reminders of the past automatically activate certain neurobiological responses explains why trauma survivors are vulnerable to react with irrational, subcortically initiated responses that are irrelevant, and even harmful, in the present....

Exposure to extreme threat, particularly early in life, combined with a lack of adequate caregiving responses, significantly affects the long-term capacity of the human organism to modulate the response of the sympathetic and parasympathetic nervous systems in response to subsequent stress.

BESSEL A. VAN DER KOLK[35]

Traumatic stress symptoms have a physiological basis. We are going to offer the reader a fairly technical overview of the body's survival response system and of the link between this adaptive system and traumatic stress symptoms. We invite you to read this section if it interests you, but feel free to skip past it if you have less interest in the body's physiological underpinnings of the trauma response.

When we are faced with a potentially threatening situation, our body's survival system kicks into gear. We respond with a variety of strategies designed to get us away from danger, including fight, flight, freeze, and submit responses.

Activation of the survival response relies upon two major systems in the body: the autonomic nervous system and the endocrine system. The autonomic nervous system is composed of the sympathetic and parasympathetic branches. The sympathetic nervous system (SNS) is designed to mobilize the body's resources in threatening or stressful situations. It signals the adrenal glands to release "stress hormones" such as epinephrine (adrenaline) and norepinephrine (noradrenaline) that prepare the body to respond to a threat. Activation of the SNS contributes to an increase in heart rate and blood pressure, acceleration in respiration, and preparation of the muscles for action. The parasympathetic nervous system turns "off" the body's activation. The balance between these two systems is essential for regulating the body's energy and directing resources to where they are needed.

The stress response also involves activation of the hypothalamus-pituitary-adrenal (HPA) axis, a neuroendocrine response system. This system involves a feedback loop that is initiated when the hypothalamus secretes corticotropin-releasing hormone (CRH), a hormone that prepares the body for action under conditions of threat. CRH causes the pituitary gland to secrete adrenocorticotropic hormone (ACTH) into your bloodstream, which then triggers your adrenal glands to release numerous hormones, including cortisol, the body's primary stress-fighting hormone.

The fight, flight, freeze, and submit response patterns are each associated with particular neurophysiological reactions in the body. The fight response is a high arousal response, suggesting activation of the SNS as well as the HPA axis. In the fight response, we are able to approach a threatening stimulus and actively work to repel it. The SNS and neuroendocrine system are also highly implicated in the flight response. When we experience a flight response, our bodies are activated to get us away from danger. The physiological response is similar to the fight response, but the emotions (anxiety and fear versus anger and rage) and the coping response (avoidance versus approach) are different.

There are indications that the freeze response involves activation of both the sympathetic and the parasympathetic nervous systems. This theory is consistent with animal models of threat response systems, which have shown coactivation of the sympathetic and parasympathetic branches in freeze-type responses to threat.[36] When we experience a freeze response, our bodies are highly activated, and we are aware of a potential threat. We are assimilating extensive sensory information from our environment in order to make a decision about how to respond. Meanwhile, we are in a hypervigilant "tonicfreeze" state: our bodies remain immobile, directing all of our available energy toward taking in information about the threatening situation.

The submit response involves shutting down the body's active defenses, or a dissociative response. In humans, this response is similar to an animal "playing dead" in the wild, and the physiological manifestations of the submit response appear to match what we know about the "defeat" response in the animal world. In the submit response, a primitive, unmyelinated vegetative vagus[37] of the parasympathetic nervous system is activated, shutting down our body's active defenses and leading to lowered blood pressure and heart rate. In a submit response, the body also produces endogenous opioids that mediate perception of pain and create alterations in sense of time, place, and reality.[38] The purpose of this response is to avoid further enraging an aggressor and to disconnect from the experience of pain associated with an attack.

Most of us use all of these survival strategies at various times, and we may use combinations of these strategies in response to a single incident. In the face of an imminent threat, each of these responses is adaptive and is designed to help us avoid, escape, or cope with dangerous situations. However, in some cases these responses begin to emerge in situations that do not involve actual threat or danger. When we are exposed to intense, chronic, or repeated traumatic events, our threat response system may become altered. Research has indicated that people who have PTSD show a sensitization of several biological systems, including a more reactive autonomic nervous system and a sensitized neuroendocrine system (HPA axis), with decreased basal cortisol levels.[39]

These alterations in the body's physiological threat response system show up as trauma-related symptoms, including overarousal or underarousal of the body. Overarousal symptoms include anxiety and fear, intrusive memories, triggered reactions, concentration problems, nightmares, and hypervigilance, among others. When our bodies are hyperaroused, we may feel on guard for signs of threat or danger or may be easily triggered into a survival response. Underarousal symptoms include emotional numbing, social avoidance, hypersomnia, fatigue and low energy, and dissociation. When we experience underarousal, our threat response system may be underactive or shut down, leading us to miss signs of potential danger. Many individuals who have experienced chronic interpersonal trauma disconnect from their bodies, so that they no longer feel emotional or physical pain. Along with the loss of pain sensations, people who regularly dissociate from their experiences often lose other physical and emotional sensations such as the experience of joy, pleasure, and connectedness. People who have experienced chronic or repeated trauma often experience dysregulation in their body's arousal systems and find themselves alternating between being highly sensitized and easily triggered, and feeling numb or disconnected from themselves and other people.

The Impact of Trauma

Trauma robs the victim of a sense of power and control.

JUDITH HERMAN, cofounder of the Victims of Violence Program at the Cambridge Health Alliance and author of *Trauma and Recovery*[40]

Emotional pain and traumatic memories can be "stored" in the body long after exposure to a traumatic situation has ended. As Bessel A. van der Kolk has described it, "the body keeps the score."[41] Storing traumatic memories, and the associated emotional tone, is evolutionarily adaptive. We need to remember dangerous or threatening situations so that we can try to avoid these situations in the future. But holding these memories in our bodies, in a physical and emotional sense, can create a great deal of discomfort and distress.

Many trauma survivors experience an ongoing battle within their bodies. Symptoms of PTSD provide one illustration of this kind of internal conflict. Two of the symptom categories of PTSD are intrusive symptoms and avoidance symptoms. Intrusive symptoms occur when memories of the traumatic event intrude into our consciousness, at times unbidden, in other instances triggered by a reminder. We might respond to these intrusive memories with emotional and/or physiological distress. In some cases, the intrusion can be so severe that we lose track of current time and place and feel as if the trauma is happening all over again (a "flashback"). Avoidance symptoms provide the counterbalance to intrusive symptoms, when we use all of our energy to try to push away the traumatic memories, to avoid reminders, and to "move on." This internal battle creates a situation of ongoing tension that is self-sustaining. Whenever the intrusions become stronger, the distress that is created leads us to increase our defenses, pushing the emotions and memories farther away. When the avoidance becomes stronger and we are able to ignore or forget the emotions and memories for some time, the intensity of the underlying emotions and memories often becomes stronger. Similar to phobic-type reactions, our avoidance actually serves to preserve and strengthen the fear and anxiety that we are trying to escape.

The most extreme form of avoidance is dissociation. Dissociation is "a compartmentalization of experience: elements of an experience are not integrated into a unitary whole but are stored in isolated fragments."[42] Dissociation is a coping mechanism used to create distance from emotions, cognitions, or somatic symptoms. When we experience ongoing danger or injury, we learn to disconnect from ourselves in order to tolerate the physical or emotional pain. Our bodies have become a place of hurt. We feel trapped within ourselves, or trapped within a world of pain. Dissociation can help us to become free of this pain. It is a mental and emotional escape.

Dissociation becomes problematic when these barriers become overly rigid, leading to fragmentation. In these cases, dissociation can create an ongoing disconnection from our emotions, body, or thoughts; can lead to significant disturbances in the continuity of our memory; and can interfere with our ability to establish an integrated sense of self. When we dissociate, we might be consciously completely unaware of traumatic memories, or of the emotional pain attached to the memories. But the pain may still be held somatically. One person might experience chronic neck and backaches from holding herself rigidly controlled. Another person might experience a choking sensation in his throat when confronted with a conflict. A third person might feel nothing in her body because she is so completely removed from the underlying pain.

All of these people might experience their bodies as "the enemy." They perceive their bodies as hurting them, because when they become conscious of the messages from their bodies, many of these messages express a sense of injury. Disconnection prevents them from hearing these painful messages. However, there is a cost to this avoidance. When we are disconnected from our bodies and from ourselves, we are not able to recognize signs of danger, which may lead to further threat or injury. We are not able to recognize the building signs of stress, and so are not able to compensate with increased self-care or to resolve the underlying issues causing the stress. Chronic stress causes a slow wearing on our minds and bodies that can compound underlying trauma-related issues. We are not able to truly connect with others because we are not in touch with ourselves. And, finally, we are missing out on the joy of being truly present and connecting with ourselves.

Yoga as Trauma Treatment

The guiding principle of recovery is restoring a sense of power and control to the survivor.
JUDITH HERMAN[43]

Because trauma affects the body's physiology, and because traumatic memories are often stored somatically, leaders in the field are increasingly insisting that trauma treatment must incorporate the body.[44]

Many types of traditional therapy rely upon a cognitive or "top-down" approach to treatment, while yoga-based interventions utilize a "bottom-up" approach that draws on somatic experience as an entryway into a person's inner life. Body-oriented therapies are based on the assumption that our minds can be "slippery": people can sometimes engage in talk therapy for years and never access important aspects of their inner experience. Intellectualization, a commonly used defense, is when we spend considerable time trying to figure something out but never get to the essence of whatever it is we are trying to work out. Body-oriented therapies such as yoga-based interventions prioritize making a connection at the somatic level, and then moving from that entry point to addressing emotions and cognitions.

Yoga-based approaches use a series of postures and breathing techniques to build a sense of connection to the self. Yoga practitioners are able to cultivate the ability to remain present, to notice and tolerate inner experience, and to develop a new relationship with their body. This body-based practice then has a ripple effect on emotional and mental health, on relationships, and on one's experience of living in the world.

three

Yoga

The Origins of Yoga

> Yoga is the path which cultures the body and senses, refines the mind, civilizes the intelligence, and takes rest in the soul which is the core of our being.
> B.K.S. IYENGAR, renowned yoga teacher and one of the first to popularize yoga in the West
> Yoga is a way of life. It changes you and therefore changes the way you relate to other people and influence your environment.
> VANDA SCARAVELLI, innovative yoga teacher, student of Iyengar, and author of *Awakening the Spine*[1]

To encapsulate the entire history of yoga is neither within our scope nor essential to the purpose of this book.[2] Instead, as we explore the origins and advancement of yoga, we will highlight particular aspects of yogic philosophy along with principles and practices that we believe are most relevant to our central concern—namely, how to make yoga accessible to survivors of severe psychological trauma.

For more than five thousand years, human beings have practiced yoga. Yoga can be traced back to some of the earliest writing to come out of the geographical areas now known as modern-day Pakistan and India—the Indus and Sarasvati Valleys. These early texts, called the Vedas and the Upanishads, are considered to be sacred literature of Hinduism. Early manifestations of yoga also appear in the meditative practices of two other world religions to originate from the region, Buddhism and Jainism.

As yoga evolved in the context of ancient India and the flourishing of Hinduism, Buddhism, and Jainism, people who considered themselves yogis (yoga practitioners) in turn borrowed characteristics from these major religions in order to create a yoga orthodoxy. There seems to have been a very organic, fluid relationship between yoga practices and philosophy and the tenets of these three major religions. One prominent yogi whose writing has survived into our time, Patanjali, compiled perhaps the most dogmatic text associated purely with yoga, borrowing from Buddhism in particular. Written in the second century BCE, his Yoga Sutras (in Hinduism, a sutra refers to a literary collection of aphorisms or truths, and translates to "a thread that holds things together") were considered both as Hindu scripture and as foundational theory on yoga philosophy and practice.[3] Delineated within this seminal work, Patanjali's "Ashtanga," also known as the "eight limbs (steps) of yoga," remains central to modern conceptualizations of the self-discipline and mindfulness involved in living a yogic lifestyle.

Despite the clear religious connection found in the history of yoga, many who have thought about, practiced, and written about yoga over the ensuing two millennia have argued that the practice of yoga itself was not developed to adhere to the strictures of a particular religion but rather is flexible enough to become incorporated into diverse religious, spiritual, or secular traditions and to be practiced according to the personal or communal needs and goals of various people over time. Many believe that yoga is first and foremost an "inquiry into being," an invitation for those curious about what it means to be alive, and not a religion. In this light, yoga is a set of ideas proposed by very sensible people as investigations into the subjective (and possibly objective) experience of being. While the early writings associated with yoga are steeped in ritual and religious dogma, yoga as a practice has survived the millennia mostly because of its expansive and inclusive nature; it has been adaptable to the needs of highly disparate cultures from ancient India to modern-day New York City. As we distill our inquiry into the origins of yoga, this inclusive and adaptable quality is central in our own efforts to modify yoga practices to be trauma-sensitive. While yoga has meant many things to many people, for the purpose of our work, we are aligned with the conceptualization of yoga not as a religion but rather as a practical inquiry into being.

Another important characteristic of the history of yoga with which we must contend is the long tradition of gurus that stems from yoga's Eastern roots but spills over into the Western embrace of yoga as a cult of personalities.[4] In the most extreme cases of this guru legacy, yoga practitioners are commanded to subjugate their will to that of the guru and to deny their own subjective experience, trusting totally in the mandates and proclivities of the teacher. For those of us interested in trauma-sensitive yoga, this is the exact opposite of what we hope for from yoga, and in fact it seems closer to a definition of trauma than a liberating practice based on self-discovery and self-care. Therefore, we reject the guru culture that can be found in yoga's past and present in favor of a model where the yoga teacher, while creating some structure and safety, invites students to listen first and foremost to their own bodies and to be guided by their own experience in the moment. There is no need for a guru or for dogma in order for the practice to be safe, effective, and even spiritually nourishing for trauma survivors.

Hopefully this inquiry has shown that yoga represents many things to many people. It is just as adaptable to those of us interested in making it available to trauma survivors as it was to those interested in using it to form the cornerstone of a spiritual practice. We can modify the yoga to suit our needs and still call it yoga because the practice has survived by being so expansive and adaptable. In fact, it could be argued that our emphasis on yoga as a practice of self-inquiry and self-care above all may actually be closer to the intentions of the first yoga practitioners than are some other modern interpretations. Regardless, yoga is sufficiently robust to survive many interpretations. Religious practitioners have been able to claim yoga, as well as lay practitioners. People looking for a prescribed path have been able to visit a guru, while those more inclined toward a self-directed approach have been equally as satisfied practicing yoga in the privacy of their living rooms.

Given the various ways of describing yoga, it would be reasonable to suggest that yoga is ultimately a practice or group of practices that can be suited to the physical, emotional, and spiritual needs of each individual practitioner. While there are myriad yoga practices advocated by a multitude of teachers, there is ultimately a yoga practice best suited for each individual, and for that individual alone. In the context of trauma-sensitive yoga, this is a helpful way to consider yoga. The intention is not to limit or prescribe experiences. The intention is to learn to be with and to interact with our own bodies in such a way that we come to know what works best for us.

While it is important to practice general guidelines for safety, and for teachers to provide clear, succinct instruction during a traumasensitive yoga class, it is at least as important for students to become comfortable with guiding and directing their own experience. This may mean learning how to stop doing something if it is painful or uncomfortable for any reason. This may mean asking a teacher for help. This may mean leaving a class and taking a walk if one becomes overwhelmed with thoughts and feelings. In the context of traumasensitive yoga, we are learning to tolerate and encourage any choices that a student makes in support of his or her own well-being. Much of this book will investigate ways of doing just this from the perspective of the practitioner, the yoga teacher, and the clinician.

Yoga in the West

Yoga is a spectacularly multifaceted phenomenon, and as such it is very difficult to define because there are exceptions to every conceivable rule.

GEORG FEUERSTEIN, PHD, author of *The Yoga Tradition,* and instrumental in translating yoga practice for a Western audience

Because our practice of trauma-sensitive yoga was developed here in the United States, it is important to consider this context in some detail.

Specifically, let's take a look at what the practice of yoga looks like today in the Western world.

According to a 2008 study called "Yoga in America" and published in the *Yoga Journal,* Americans spend $5.7 billion a year on yoga classes and products, including equipment, clothing, vacations, and media (DVDs, videos, books, and magazines).[5] This same study indicated that 15.8 million Americans practice yoga and that an additional 18.3 million are "extremely interested" in yoga.

Anyone interested in practicing yoga in a major U.S. city will probably not have far to go. A quick web search will likely identify a nearby yoga studio, community center, or health club offering a variety of yoga classes. For the most part, all of the classes will be similar in that they will be characterized by the use of postures and breathing exercises. During that web search, the curious will also notice, however, that there are many different styles of yoga to choose from, with some of the most popular being Vinyasa, Power, Iyengar, and Bikram, among dozens of others. While all of these emphasize the physical practice and attention to breath, each style presents yoga in a slightly different way. For example, some styles are more focused on postural alignment, while others concentrate on synchronizing movement and breath.

In order to understand why yoga needs to be modified for trauma survivors, let's consider in detail some of the most popular styles found in your average American city. In doing this, we will be making some generalizations based on our own experiences. There are always exceptions to the rule. Also, as we consider some key characteristics of these popular styles, we will begin to indicate where trauma survivors have found significant challenges in order to move us toward a detailed examination of why and how we modify yoga in order for it to be trauma-sensitive.

Bikram[6] and most Power[7] yoga classes are taught with the heat turned up to around 100 degrees. You break into a sweat just walking into the room. This has an effect on what practitioners wear during these classes—not much! Men often go shirtless, and otherwise there tends to be an abundance of spandex and tank tops. Sweating is pervasive and profuse, and quarters may be uncomfortably close, depending on how many people are in the room.

Along with these physical dynamics, there is also a characteristic language that teachers of Power and Bikram yoga tend to use during the classes. Power yoga instructors emphasize "holding just a little longer," "pushing just a little farther," or "taking it a little deeper." There is a whole array of language that goes with these concepts, but the most important point for us is that students will likely be guided toward pushing their bodies instead of listening closely to them. In Bikram classes, the language, along with the sequence, is almost totally prearranged.

If students try something different from what the teacher has instructed, they may be publicly corrected, which some students have told us feels as if they are being chastised or scolded. Instructors tend to give very specific directions about how a form is to be done, and there may be very little room for self-exploration based on the language used by the instructor of a Bikram yoga class.

The styles described above have some characteristics that new students may not be aware of before walking into the room, but which bear greatly on their experience in the room. We recognize that trauma often involves the experience of being pushed, coerced, or forced—having someone or something else in a position of power attempt to usurp control of one's body. Many trauma survivors have experienced a somatic sense of helplessness. They often have deep reservations about whether they could ever feel in control of themselves or experience their bodies in a positive way. The dynamics described above in these yoga classes can very easily fit into that paradigm and, for the traumatized person, may actually reinforce a sense of powerlessness and ineffectiveness.

What happens when the person in authority says, "Hold this just a little longer," but your experience is that it is uncomfortable and even painful to do so? Many people we work with at the Trauma Center have described this as a profound dilemma. They often say they were not ready to listen to their own body and ended up following the teacher's instructions and hurting themselves in some way. This is exactly what we work to avoid in our trauma-sensitive yoga classes and in integrating yoga-based strategies in therapy. The priority clearly shifts to the students learning to listen to their own bodies and making choices that involve taking care of themselves.

Another very popular yoga style in the West is Iyengar.[8] Named after its founder, B.K. S Iyengar, this style is very goal-oriented and emphasizes "correct alignment." Along with the strong focus on alignment, which can seem arbitrary and externally imposed rather than directed toward trusting the internal perspective of the student, many Iyengar teachers use a wide array of props, including in some cases an entire wall of straps and rubber cords. A number of our students have experienced being tied down or physically restrained in some way as part of their trauma, and for them that strap is not a helpful yoga tool, but a torture device. Because of feedback from our brave students, we no longer keep straps at the Trauma Center. It became clear to us that the potential benefit of the yoga strap was negligible in comparison to our students feeling safe in the room.

A further challenge with a prop-heavy yoga practice like Iyengar is that students are directed (not asked) to use several props in order to get a posture right, and this can give the message that one's bodily experience needs to be mediated by external objects in order to be correct. While using props can be a fun and very useful experiment if it is self-directed, if not skillfully introduced, it can reinforce the feeling that the body is a problem that needs correcting. This can become a harmful message in the context of trauma recovery, where much of the healing involves trusting, accepting, and appreciating one's body as it is.

Finally, Vinyasa[9] classes tend to emphasize movement between postures, which can get pretty fast, depending on the particular teacher. It can be very easy to get lost in a Vinyasa class, quickly fall behind, and feel like you need to catch up in order to "do it right." Falling behind the instructor and other students can reinforce a sense of failure and inadequacy and can lead to giving up entirely rather than suffering that humiliation again. We have also had students at the Trauma Center tell us that a Vinyasa-style class actually provided an opportunity to dissociate because the rhythm was so brisk that they would "check out" entirely and sometimes forget where they were or what happened once the class was over. With trauma-sensitive yoga we hope to help people maintain mindfulness throughout the practice so that they are building affect regulation skills. This involves finding a pace—not too slow, not too fast—at which folks can safely notice where they are and experience breathing and moving in a safe, effective way.

Class style has a profound effect on the experience, and we need to consider which characteristics are beneficial and which are distracting, detrimental, or dangerous as we investigate trauma-sensitive yoga. Another important variable to every yoga class are the teachers themselves. In this context, there is one key dynamic to consider, and that is whether or not the teacher does physical assists. That is, how likely is a yoga teacher to use his or her body as a way of adjusting a student's form? It is our observation that yoga teachers in the West generally tend to overutilize physical assists. Some teachers learn to ask permission first, but many, in the interest of time or for some other reason, will have their hands on a student before the practitioner is even aware that the teacher is approaching.

For many trauma survivors, from the military veteran to the survivor of sexual abuse, having people put their hands on you out of the blue and without asking permission is a recipe for disaster. Consider this common example. Many folks have told us of being in a yoga class, in a position like Downward-Facing Dog (picture an upside-down V), and the teacher comes up from behind and puts his hand between the student's shoulder blades and pushes down. While the intention may be good, the effect can be a serious trigger leading to a flashback or dissociation, and that may be the last yoga class for the student. We will return to the topic of physical assists, including some of our recommendations regarding assists, later in the book.

Obviously, what we consider to be significant challenges for trauma survivors has not had an effect on the overall success of yoga in the West. Along with becoming a multi-billion-dollar business, yoga is part of our popular psyche. From the Beatles to Madonna, to episodes of *Sex in the City* and much more, yoga has permeated Western culture. Many people find standard yoga classes to be extremely enjoyable and helpful. Still, our special concern in this book is with trauma survivors. We believe that because of some of the characteristics of the most popular yoga styles available to the average "consumer," trauma survivors have not had equal access to the potential benefits that yoga has to offer. For many trauma survivors, yoga has been another condition for failure, disappointment, and pain.[10]

In the sections that follow, we will present some key modifications that we make to yoga classes so that they are trauma-sensitive. We will offer some suggestions and an at-home practice specifically for survivors. Later sections will be directed to clinicians who wish to introduce basic elements of yoga into the therapy office or the milieu setting (providers working with groups at schools, hospitals, refugee camps, community centers, and other such places) and to yoga teachers who are interested in creating a trauma-sensitive yoga class. Though we have broken the information down in this way, we intend for all of the sections to be useful to anyone, especially trauma survivors, who want to understand why we believe certain modifications are indicated and indeed necessary in order to make yoga trauma-sensitive.

four

Trauma-Sensitive Yoga

The Need for Trauma-Sensitive Yoga

In recent years, an emerging research literature has started to demonstrate the importance of helping patients with the management of current problems with dissociation, affect regulation, and altered relationships with themselves and others prior to engaging them in trauma exposure [more traditional talk therapy].

BESSEL A. VAN DER KOLK, MD

I do not view post-traumatic stress disorder as a pathology to be managed, suppressed, or adjusted to, but the result of a natural process gone awry. Healing trauma requires a direct experience of the living, feeling, knowing organism.

PETER A. LEVINE, PHD

The practice of yoga only requires us to act and to be attentive in our actions.

T.K.V DESIKACHAR, influential yoga teacher and author of *The Heart of Yoga*

Trauma has a deep and long-lasting effect on the entire organism, from chemical and anatomical changes in the brain, to changes in our body's physiological systems, to the subjective impact on the experience of the survivor.[1] We believe that treatment for trauma must be equally thorough—considering the person as a whole and addressing the broad-ranging effects of trauma on an individual. It also needs to meet the intensity of the traumatic sequelae with an equal measure of patience, compassion, and gentleness. If we are to help people recover from the insidious violation of their humanity that is trauma, we must be able to offer a varied array of tools to aid in this task. At the Trauma Center, we are beginning to understand how yoga can serve as one particularly effective tool for helping trauma survivors on their often long and complex path to recovery.

In order for yoga to be effective, folks have to practice it, which can create a challenge. Clearly, for many survivors of trauma, the body is at best disconnected from the self and, at worst, is a volatile, dangerous place. Yoga is fundamentally a body-based activity, so we reach an impasse: how can we make this body-based activity accessible and tolerable when the body has become the enemy?

At the Trauma Center Yoga Program, we devote extensive time to exploration of this question. In every class that we teach, we see brave women and men who want desperately to heal, but who are in obvious distress sitting, standing, or just being. Every stilted movement, every rigid gesture expresses this deep struggle: I have learned that my body is the enemy, but in order for me to live this life now, I must find a way to befriend my body.

If you are a yoga teacher offering yoga classes to trauma survivors, please pause and recognize how brave it is for your students just to show up in the room. If you are a clinician offering some gentle yoga exercises in your office, you know how heroic it is for your client to try moving and breathing in a gentle, mindful way. If you are a trauma survivor trying yoga for the first time (or the hundredth time!), and it seems way more difficult than you ever imagined it would be, you are not alone. Please take a moment to consider Kate's story as a way of understanding what a typical yoga class might be like for a survivor of trauma.

Kate's Story

Kate (an amalgam of several students we have had over the years) is a survivor of chronic childhood sexual abuse from within her family. She hears about a local yoga studio and is intrigued—terrified, but intrigued. After months of looking at the studio's website, having memorized the weekly schedule and the biographies of the teachers, she chooses the teacher whom she feels will be the best fit for her, and she writes down on her calendar for Friday afternoon, "yoga class, 4PM."

Kate lives alone but has a longtime therapist. She has talked with her therapist about yoga, but she has not discussed how deeply gut-wrenching the whole decision process has been for her. She doesn't have the words for it. She is young, and by nature physically fit, but has never tried any kind of group sport or activity since one disastrous semester of volleyball in high school.

Friday afternoon comes, and with the sheer energy of youth (and even then just barely) she shows up at the yoga studio at 3:40. In some circles (trauma-sensitive therapists and yoga teachers to name two), this could be considered a miracle. We know how difficult it is for Kate to come to this public place where people will be acknowledging their bodies! It's one thing at the university where she moves from one task to another, focused on logical solutions to problems, or at the lab where she is considered one of the brightest young scientists in her field. In these settings, she is just a brain—a highly functioning brain, and this feels comfortable for her. She does not have a body; she is not a whole being.

When she enters the yoga studio, she is greeted at the front desk by a young woman, just about her age. "Welcome," she says gently with a smile (good!). Kate pays and is oriented to the space where the class will take place, "Shoes go here; changing room is there" (good!). Kate notices that the yoga room has incense burning, which makes her feel physically ill. She sees that there is one wall in the room with straps and belts hanging from it, and this makes her very uncomfortable. The young woman behind the desk says some other things that whiz by, unnoticed by Kate, but then there is something about telling the teacher if there are any noteworthy physical injuries. (What is that? Injuries—where to begin?) Kate says, "No injuries," and proceeds to get set up for the class. She purposely chose a sixty-minute class instead of a longer one in order to "try it all out." She sets her mat up near the door because she feels that it is very important that she be within a few feet of the door.

The class begins, and the next hour is a long one. Many things happen, but really only two things "happen." The first is that, within ten minutes, the teacher (the same kind, young woman from the front desk) has come up behind Kate during a posture called Child's Pose and has put her hand gently between Kate's shoulder blades. Kate's forehead is on the floor, and for a split second when the teacher's hand is on her body, she cannot lift her head. She knows logically that it only lasted for a second or so, but it felt like forever. The teacher had called Child's Pose a "safe" place to be, but it wasn't safe for Kate any longer.

At some point later (maybe a few minutes, or maybe ... who knows how long?), she heard the teacher say, "Maybe we should do what we dread." The words were in some form or another—the form doesn't matter so much—but all Kate heard was that instruction, "Maybe we should do what we dread." The teacher was smiling, light-hearted when delivering this line, but for Kate, there was darkness. There was almost uncontrollable rage, suddenly controlled without thought, but then ... fear, and incredible, profound loneliness. There was no concept of time. Kate had come to recognize what was happening as dissociation, a very familiar experience for her but still frightening and out of her control. There had been many times where she had woken up in some man's bedroom, having no recollection of how she ended up there—this experience was similar.

In this case, Kate did recognize where the door was, and she left. She got her stuff, and she left before anyone could talk with her. The teacher may have thought she was just leaving to go to the bathroom or to get a drink of water, but she was leaving for good. Outside the studio, she called her therapist.

Kate's story is so typical. Yoga is ubiquitous these days in any major metropolitan area (and beyond), and the promise of yoga to help one develop a kind, gentle relationship with one's body is part of the zeitgeist. Yoga promises peace of body and mind, but there is so much that goes on during a typical yoga class that can be devastating for some trauma survivors.

In setting out to establish the Trauma Center Yoga Program, we felt that there was a way to make the yoga experience safer for survivors of trauma. We wanted folks like Kate to discover an interest in yoga and then have a safe place where they could truly begin to befriend their bodies through the yoga practice.

To get us started, here are some broad statements regarding trauma-sensitive yoga. Trauma-sensitive yoga is body oriented (physical) and down-to-earth but does not deny the needs of the spirit. It is skills-based but not cold or joyless. It is structured but emphasizes choice. Shifting our relationship to our selves is a slow process that takes patience and repetition. A trauma-sensitive yoga practice can provide a structured approach that helps foster our internal sense of safety, personal agency, and choice and that cultivates our capacity for self-awareness and self-regulation.[2]

Key Themes of Trauma-Sensitive Yoga

We have identified four main themes that have emerged as particularly important for yoga with trauma survivors: experiencing the present moment, making choices, taking effective action, and creating rhythms.

These themes have been developed by yoga instructors working in conjunction with clinicians, so we consider them to be clinically informed. As an example, Bessel A. van der Kolk, founder and medical director of the Trauma Center, often refers to trauma as "a disease of not being able to be present." This characterization led to the articulation of the first of our four themes. Yoga teachers can build an entire class or curriculum around a single theme. Alternately, they can integrate trauma-sensitive practices in the way we most often strive to do in our own work with survivors, which is to touch on each of the four themes in the course of one class. The themes will naturally blend into one another, and yoga teachers will find their own trauma-sensitive language that helps them to sharpen or clarify the material to suit their specific students.

Experiencing the Present Moment

I wanted to bring in yoga for many reasons. The first is because due to the past trauma, so many of these kids are so separated from their bodies and their understanding of their bodies. With regulation skills practiced in yoga, the kids are invited to read their body cues, understand their reactions—this is hard to do when they are so separated from their bodies. In addition, so much of their lives are fast paced, including the other physical activities we offer. Yoga allows a way to slowly build strength, which illustrates one of our core missions.

CLINICIAN offering trauma-sensitive yoga to youth

Consider this statement from Dr. van der Kolk: "The goal of treatment of PTSD is to help people live in the present, without feeling or behaving according to irrelevant demands belonging to the past."[3] Some reasons why survivors might struggle with being present (itself a possibly familiar but potentially elusive concept) have already been speculated upon in this book. We might say that as a result of the body's natural survival systems, many trauma survivors are fundamentally oriented toward the trauma, and not to what is happening right now. To simplify, imagine a combat veteran at a restaurant, having dinner. A car backfires outside. When the car backfires, the combat veteran is no longer having dinner at a safe bistro in the South End of Boston but is physiologically and emotionally back in the war zone, being fired upon. It is suddenly a matter of life and death.[4] Readers may be able to imagine many other similar scenarios that might catapult a survivor out of relationship to the present (what is actually happening right now) and fling them into feeling and behaving according to demands belonging to the past (the traumatic event or events). This is a very difficult way to live. Learning to live in the present means shifting the orientation from the trauma to the now, and it can be terrifying for many survivors to "let their guard down" in this manner. Most traumasensitive clinicians explore a variety of strategies and techniques with their clients to help them learn to live in the present. In this context we consider yoga to be an unparalleled practice for helping us to be somatically present. Let's consider an example of a deceptively simple, yoga-based present-moment experience that occurred at the Trauma Center.

AWARENESS OF BREATH

After two yoga classes, Cathy told her therapist that she was aware of her breath for the first time. She realized that when she held her breath, she felt more anxious, and when she allowed herself to breathe more fully, her body began to relax. She was smiling when she conveyed this information. After decades of therapy, the fact that Cathy was not aware of her breath had never come up. Now that her therapist and especially Cathy herself knew

(1) that she had not been aware of her breath before and (2) that she could now notice her body in this way in the present moment, new pathways were opened up in terms of therapy. She was able to make connections between her somatic sensations and her emotions. This mindful practice also provided her with a safe, positive, body-based present-moment experience.

If Cathy has found a way to have a present-moment experience that she can practice with her therapist, with her yoga teacher, and on her own, she may have discovered a tool that helps her stay present when she most needs it—when a trigger comes, and she is pulled into relationship with the past in a way that feels out of her control. We are inclined to trust such a simple practice as being aware of one's breath as a legitimate present-moment experience that may be very useful as a coping tool to manage dissociation. On a deeper level, the potential significance of Cathy's observation as a foundational step toward somatic awareness and regulation cannot be overlooked.

For many individuals that we have worked with, the somatic dissociation is even deeper. Yoga teachers and clinicians can use physical cues to help survivors make links to their present-moment experience. For example, in Mountain posture, the teacher might invite students to bring their feet flat on the floor and then to take a moment to experiment with feeling their feet on the ground. One helpful instruction for us has been, "Maybe there are some things you can do to help you feel your feet on the ground, like move your toes, or gently tap your heels."

We consider present-moment experience to be physical and body-based, not intellectual or theoretical. We want to provide students with as many opportunities as possible to have these kinds of experiences in a trauma-sensitive yoga class so that they may begin to experience being present. For some folks that we've worked with, their somatic dissociation is even deeper. Frank, a man in his midfifties, talked about a present-moment experience that he had in a yoga class at the Trauma Center. Through this class, he became aware that he had been living his life completely cut off from the experience of his body.

FRANK'S STORY

When Frank came to his first yoga class at the Trauma Center, the teacher invited the class to experiment with some seated leg lifts. This exercise involved sitting in a chair in a comfortable upright position and extending one leg at a time (feel free to try this yourself if you like). After a few minutes of investigating lifting, holding, breathing, and returning back to a neutral seated form, the teacher asked the students, "What did you notice?" Frank replied that he had no idea he was lifting his leg unless he was looking at it. For both the teacher and for Frank, this was a true moment of discovery. Frank had been in therapy for a couple of decades because of his PTSD symptoms, but he had never been asked about his somatic sensations: Are you aware of your body? Can you feel yourself moving? Do you feel disconnected from your physical self? It had never occurred to him or to his therapists that it might be important for Frank to investigate this fundamental relationship to his body.

To be fair, traditional therapy is not oriented toward this kind of inquiry. Traditional therapy is geared more toward talking about events, thoughts, or feelings, rather than actually experiencing movement and sensations in the moment. Frank was able to *talk* about his experiences for years, without *experiencing* an awareness of the present moment. He realized that he had actually been using the talking as a way of disconnecting with his experiencing—instead just telling his story over and over in a disconnected way.

As we have seen in this book, the traditional therapeutic paradigm has been shifting more and more in recent years, and now many trauma-informed clinicians work with their clients at the somatic level. Clinicians and clients are getting up and moving around the office and investigating what is noticed and felt right in the moment. For Frank, this simple leg lift in a yoga class was a first opportunity for this type of inquiry.

The next step in the process was equally as important. The yoga teacher invited Frank to both look at his leg as he was lifting it and place one hand on top of his thigh as he was lifting and releasing his leg. When the teacher asked the students to be curious about how the experience was different when they applied some pressure to their upper leg, Frank realized that he could feel the muscles in his quadriceps (the big muscles on the top of the thigh) tightening. Frank shared this experience with his therapist, and he practiced lifting and releasing his leg while both looking at it and placing a hand on the quadriceps. He worked with his therapist on noticing both the somatic sensations and the emotions that he experienced during this present-moment experience. This became a very successful way for Frank to begin to reconnect to interoception, or feeling his own body. As time went on, he was surprised that he was able to feel his legs moving without looking at them.

Frank's story brings up a number of questions. What did this experience offer Frank?

Now that Frank had a way to interact with the muscular dynamics in his legs, how would this change his relationship to his body? How would this impact his process of healing? These are great questions for survivors, clinicians, and yoga teachers to ask each other and ourselves as we are experimenting with yoga-based interventions. These are questions that echo throughout this book and that are right at the heart of the work.

Making Choices

Trauma is an experience of having no choice. Whether you are a soldier being attacked in battle, a child in an abusive home, or a woman walking alone who is assaulted, your choice about what happened to you did not matter. This profound lack of choice is a common denominator among trauma survivors. It connects the person who is stuck in a riptide, the woman who is abused by her domestic partner, the marine under enemy fire, and the child who is being bullied. Something terrible happened that severely undermined our sense of agency in the world. Something happened that can make us seriously doubt, with good cause, that we have any control at all over what happens to us in this world. Fear and a sense of helplessness can stop people from being active participants in their lives. We believe that part of the process of healing from trauma involves regaining this sense of agency and a felt sense of control. Whether it's a Model Mugging[5] course for the rape survivor or a civilian return trip to Vietnam for the veteran, there are opportunities out there for making choices about how to confront trauma-related symptoms and how to develop a sense of empowerment.

We believe that yoga can be helpful for similar reasons, but there is something else that yoga can do. Along with a total lack of choice, trauma is characterized by extreme violence: war, rape, domestic abuse, car accidents, the profound deprivation of chronic childhood neglect and withholding of safe love and affection—these are all terribly violent experiences. Some of the clients we work with have benefited from aspects of physical practices that involve self-defense and combat training; they find in these a source of empowerment and strength. The capacity to benefit from such practices, however, almost always occurs, if at all, at a relatively advanced stage in one's recovery from trauma. In contrast, we have consistently observed that the majority of survivors of chronic maltreatment and neglect that we serve are unable to safely engage such techniques or tolerate the violent and painful memories and associated traumatic thoughts, emotions, and bodily responses that activation of aggressive action patterns, even in the interest of self-defense, routinely triggers. Trauma survivors need to find ways to be in their bodies in a gentle, nurturing way. What trauma-sensitive yoga offers that is distinct from many other physical practices is a structured, supportive, and self-paced medium for survivors to make choices in relation to their bodies and their experience that are kind, gentle, and caring—all of the things that were missing during the trauma.

Making choices to be kind, gentle, and caring toward ourselves takes practice for all of us, but for trauma survivors it is of particular importance. Yoga offers a way to practice making small, manageable choices in relation to one's body. For example, in neck rolls, the teacher may point out that students may come into contact with some muscles that are very tight or tense. The teacher may emphasize that students have choices in relation to those sensations: "If it is painful, you can always stop." This is a central aspect to empowerment for each person: if there is ever any pain or discomfort in your yoga practice, you can always stop what you are doing. Implied here is, "You are not stuck in this painful experience just because I introduced this neck roll to you. If you do not like the experience for any reason, you have control—you can stop." This kind of choice making can take considerable time for students, clinicians, and yoga teachers to accept and trust. Everyone involved—clinician, yoga teacher, and students—will benefit from much patience and repetition of these kinds of instructions.

Once the primary choice to stop at any point has been established, the yoga teacher may want to point out that there are other choices as well. Students may want to experiment with making the movement smaller to see if that allows them to keep moving but without any pain or discomfort. Students may wish to explore the stretch and make the movement a little bigger. The teacher can reiterate multiple times throughout each class that students always have choices with what they are doing with their bodies in the yoga class. The feedback we have received from many of our students is that we cannot remind them enough that they have choice. Feel free to try the neck roll exercise that follows with special attention to the practice of making choices.

NECK ROLLS FOR THE PRACTICE OF MAKING CHOICES

Please find a comfortable seat. If you like, give yourself a moment to sit up a little taller, perhaps by allowing a gentle lift through the crown of your head, the very top of your head. Take a moment to get a feeling for your naturally tall spine. You may notice some of the muscles in your body that support your tall, upright posture. When you are ready, gently release your chin toward your sternum. Just allow your chin to drop slightly toward your heart. If you like, experiment with some neck rolls. You can roll gently from side to side. Notice that you have total control over what you are doing with your body. You can make the movements very small. You can make them bigger. You can make the movements very slow. You can speed the movements up, seeing what works for you. This gesture can become a full head circle. Or maybe you lift your chin a little bit on each side. Again, feel free to investigate, making choices that suit your experience. Feel free to continue with your neck rolls for thirty seconds to a minute. Bring the exercise to an end as you are ready.

For new students, you might consider offering a small range of specific choices at first so students do not get overwhelmed. For many trauma survivors who have endured long stretches of their life that were largely devoid of choice, the invitation to make open-ended, unspecified choices is likely to be unfamiliar and can in itself engender distrust, provoke anxiety, or induce a limbic or dissociative survival response. Gradually and incrementally over time, however, our goal is to establish the frame that the students have control over what they are doing. Instructions can contribute to this felt sense of choice, as in, "Feel free to change what you are doing with this form in any way that makes you feel more comfortable." That is a big, broad instruction that may be totally overwhelming to new students, but over time it can be perfectly appropriate in the context of this practice of making choices.

The story below demonstrates how practice making choices is an important part of a trauma-sensitive yoga class.

PRACTICE MAKING CHOICES: A TEENAGER'S STORY

Similarly to their adult counterparts, children and adolescents who have experienced traumatic stress often struggle to connect to, organize, tolerate, and modulate somatic and physiological experiences.[6] Recognition of the impact of complex trauma on a physiological level has led clinicians to explore alternative methods of working with children to help them be able to notice and regulate experiences in their bodies.[7] However, trauma-sensitive yoga with children and teens may present some unique challenges. For instance, teenagers are commonly strongly influenced by their peers and concerned with self-presentation. The complexity of meaning-making and self-appraisal regarding peer status, connection, and social approval are often exponentially more complicated for traumatized youth.

A young client in her early teens was participating in a trauma-informed yoga class for girls offered in the residential school where she resided with approximately twenty other teenaged girls and boys. This young woman—we will refer to her as "Abby"—was determined to try a yoga posture that was causing her pain, seemingly just because other kids were able to achieve this posture. Abby had a strong personality and was well liked and respected by her peers, but she was also very competitive when it came to the yoga class. She gritted her teeth and began to manipulate her body forcibly toward the form.

The yoga teacher observed that Abby was holding her breath and was pushing herself too hard; however, the teacher's options were limited: there was an understanding that there would be no physical assists in this class, and the teacher was committed to this principle. If necessary, the teacher knew that she could discontinue the exercise or the class altogether, as the ultimate priority as a trauma-informed yoga instructor is to respond in a manner that preserves the safety of participants. The instructor carefully weighed the risks of Abby's forcing this particular posture against the impact of her losing this opportunity for choice, and against the risk that stopping the exercise or class could potentially activate a trauma-based constellation of affect states, self-attributions, and somatic responses related to experiences of personal failure, external control, and negative peer comparison. Knowing the form, and knowing that the physical consequences would not be dire, the teacher judged that the best thing to do was to remind Abby in a gentle, clear, and repetitive manner that she had choices and that if she felt any discomfort in her body, she could always stop. Even though these prompts were delivered close to Abby and in a soft tone of voice, they did not go unnoticed by the other students in the class, who, like many trauma survivors, were highly attuned to any indication of potential danger or threat. Not surprisingly, several of these peers and friends of Abby echoed the teacher's guidance to Abby, encouraging her not to feel compelled to complete this form. Despite these efforts, Abby was determined and continued to struggle to complete the form.

"Ow!" Abby finally exclaimed. Although she eventually stopped what she had been doing, Abby now experienced pain for the remainder of the class from having placed too much strain on her ankle. In the context of trauma-sensitive yoga, Abby made a choice: she attempted this posture through force, and it resulted in pain. Clearly, her yoga teacher could not know what Abby was feeling while she was pushing herself. Though she seemed to be uncomfortable, Abby had refused to heed invitations and reminders to modify the behavior that was causing her pain. This was difficult for the yoga teacher and for Abby's peers to witness ... but the story does not end here.

After class the yoga teacher checked in with Abby. Even though she denied any persistence of physical pain from the exercise, Abby appeared downcast and slumped in her posture, uncharacteristically avoiding eye contact. Abby agreed to discuss the experience with her individual therapist, with whom the yoga instructor would also touch base. The teacher also checked in briefly with the other students in the class to gauge their reaction to the incident, assess for the presence of any immediate safety concerns, and encourage students to bring any important material into their ongoing individual therapy. The yoga instructor subsequently updated the program's clinical director about the incident, and over the next week the program's clinical team decided on an overall response that they felt would be most helpful and least stigmatizing to all students enrolled in the residential school, whether or not they participated in the trauma-informed yoga class. Specifically, they would incorporate into the yoga classes an emphasis on "listening to the body" to more precisely examine the ways in which our bodies communicate important messages to us, the reasons and potential consequences of not listening, and the challenges and benefits of responding to the needs communicated by our bodies.

At the same time, Abby began to explore with her therapist the meaning behind her choices in yoga class and to identify some of the functions that pushing herself served for her, particularly in the presence of her peers. Abby was quickly able to recognize and label how important it was to her sense of self-esteem to be perceived as a leader and role model by her peers. In this context, the value of setting an example around self-care and setting personal limits, even when setting these limits means not being the best at something, crystallized for her. With the help of her therapist, Abby and her yoga teacher worked out an arrangement whereby Abby would lead some of the yoga exercises for an upcoming group.

On her own, without being prompted by the yoga teacher or anyone else, Abby reminded her peers several times during the class, "You can always stop if it hurts," and she ended up leading a very gentle, safe yoga class. When she finished, she was beaming ... almost as brightly, incidentally, as was a certain yoga teacher sitting toward the back of the room.

Learning to listen to her body and to make healthy choices in relation to signals from her body has continued to be a very important part of the yoga practice for Abby. Although she is still naturally inclined to push herself (a tendency that is inherently complex because it serves as both a risk and an important source of strength and resilience), over the course of the year, Abby became less likely to force her body in ways that create stress and pain. Leading her peers safely proved to be a particularly effective way for Abby to practice making choices and taking care of herself as well as her peers. Her leadership with her peers is also relevant to the third key theme, taking effective action. As you are reading that section, you may wish to review Abby's story to consider how she used her experience with making choices to empower herself to take effective action. Though it is not easy for her, Abby continues to work on making healthy choices. She is incrementally building the essential self-capacities of awareness and control over what is happening in and with her body so that she can make important choices for herself that have real and immediate consequences in her life.

Taking Effective Action

Along with a lack of choice, traumatic situations often involve experiences where all of our energy is directed toward getting away from a threat, but for some reason we cannot escape. When we are threatened, our hormones, muscles, and breath all rally, but sometimes we are not able to protect ourselves, and terrible things happen. We are pinned under the car.

We are in charge of a checkpoint in Baghdad, and a car is coming at us without stopping. We are a young child in an abusive home, watching our parent passed out on the couch. If you like, please take a moment to reflect on the experience of being stuck in a very dangerous, life-threatening circumstance. What might this feel like in your body? Can you identify sensation associated with the idea of being trapped and unable to protect yourself? A primary reason that our bodies manufacture and secrete adrenaline is to get us to move—fast. But we cannot move. The only reason for our accelerated breathing and heart rate is so our muscles can get extra oxygen so we can get away. What happens when we cannot get away, when our body's natural protective response cannot be completed? Long after the traumatic event has passed, many survivors repeatedly find themselves in frozen states in which they are unable to engage their bodies and minds to confront threatening or stressful situations.

What can we do in the context of trauma-informed yoga to help people who have experienced such helplessness to redevelop an ability to take effective action? It may begin with small, manageable steps in the context of a single yoga posture. Please consider the following practice as one such first step toward taking effective action.

PRACTICE TAKING EFFECTIVE ACTION

If you like, take a moment to notice where you are right now. Take a look around you and notice some of the characteristics of your present experience. Are you sitting in a chair? Are you sitting on a beach? Are you lying down? Are you alone? Are you in the middle of a public space? Is there a lot of noise around you? Or is it relatively quiet? How do you feel in your body? Do you feel hot or cold? Do your arms and legs feel restless, heavy, tense, relaxed? Is there a window open? Are you sitting in direct sunlight? Take a moment to notice some of the characteristics of your current experience. If you notice an area of discomfort—temperature, sensation in your lower back, too much noise—see if there is one thing you can do to make yourself feel better. If possible, pick something simple and tangible that you can do like closing a window, moving out of the sun, shifting in your chair, or moving to a quieter space: just one thing that you can do to make yourself feel better. Notice any differences that occur after you have taken this action. Are there any changes in your thoughts, your mood, your body? If you like, give this practice a moment, and then bring it to an end as you are ready.

While the above example did not involve any formal yoga postures, hopefully it gives a sense of what it might be like to practice taking effective action. This practice can occur in many ways in a trauma-sensitive yoga class. For example, at the Trauma Center we invite students from their very first class to let the instructor know if the room becomes too hot or too cold, and to then either stand up and walk across the room to open or close a window themselves or ask the teacher to do so. As another example, we have blankets and yoga blocks available in the Trauma Center yoga room that students are invited to use at any point during the class. These supports are placed where students can either get them for themselves or ask the teacher for assistance. We believe that in every yoga class, the trauma-informed teacher can create opportunities for students to create a sense of self-efficacy, and to do something to make themselves feel better. Whether this involves asking for help or doing something to help ourselves, the theme of taking effective action entails *actively doing things* that make us feel better, safer, more comfortable, or in control. In a trauma-sensitive yoga class we are honoring, and doing our best to cultivate, opportunities for students to take effective action.

Creating Rhythms

Dys-synchrony and disconnection can be major struggles for folks who have experienced complex trauma. Synchrony refers to being in sync, in step, or in rhythm. Things that are synchronous move and flow together without effort. Many survivors have spoken to us about feeling out of step with other people, and at odds with themselves.

We attend to rhythms in a trauma-sensitive yoga class because so many of the clients that we serve at the Trauma Center experience this lack of synchrony. Dissociation can create a sense of disconnection with our bodies or with the world around us. One student described dissociation as feeling like she was living behind a wall of smoked glass. The glass was sometimes so dark that she could just barely make out forms on the other side. Sometimes she could hear a voice responding to her voice; sometimes she could see some movements behind the glass; but she could not make out other people's facial expressions. She could not touch them. She was separated from the world. As Dr. Judith Herman explains, "trauma isolates." Life is often lived behind a veil that cuts trauma survivors off from the rhythmical dance and exchange that characterizes human relationship. Yoga is one way that we can experience being in sync with other people, through breath, movement, and shared experience.

Clients at the Trauma Center have also described struggling with somatic dissociation, such as Frank, who watched his legs doing leg lifts but felt that they were not a part of his body. Somatic dissociation can create disturbances in our own internal rhythms and experiences. Many of the clients who come to our center unconsciously hold their breath and have constant muscular tension. At the same time, they are unaware of feeling any tension or discomfort. This creates a lack of synchrony between their body's physiology and their felt emotions. The frozen physical state also interferes with being able to respond in a fluid way to new situations that arise; in this way, their experience is the opposite of "going with the flow."

Many survivors have talked with us about the disturbances they experience in their biorhythms—that is, the basic rhythms of life, such as eating, sleeping, and energy. Dysregulation in these rhythms means that some survivors will feel tense and keyed up all the time. Some of us will forget to eat because we have become disconnected from our body's natural rhythmic messages that we need to seek nourishment. We might feel exhausted, no matter how much sleep we get, or we might wake up repeatedly throughout the night or be unable to fall asleep. Adam, an Iraq War veteran in his early twenties (actually an amalgam of several Iraq and

Afghanistan War veterans), described the impaired biorhythms (particularly sleep disturbance) and emotional dysregulation (especially anger) that he dealt with after returning home.

ADAM'S STORY

When Adam returned from his third deployment in Iraq, he was diagnosed with PTSD. However, what mattered most to Adam was not the diagnosis, per se, but two somatic experiences that he was struggling with: he could barely sleep, and he was having frequent episodes of overwhelming rage that would come on hard and fast in an unpredictable and uncontrollable way. For both problems, Adam was prescribed medications. At one point, he was taking twelve different medications to manage these two somatic issues. For the sleep problem, Adam was prescribed several different sleeping medications that often worked in terms of knocking him out, but he would wake up groggy and not feeling rested at all. In fact, Adam described his sleep deprivation as getting worse and worse and noted that, as a result, he was feeling less and less like himself. When asked to elaborate, he said that taking the medications made him feel even more "out of control" than the initial symptoms did. Adam was a marine, and he loved the feeling of power and control that he had experienced as a marine. In the past, he had felt like he could meet any challenge successfully, and now he was relying on medications rather than on himself, which was undermining his sense of efficacy. Adam also noted that the medications and the sleep deprivation made it very difficult for him to participate in his traditional psychotherapy; as a result, he felt that he was not getting as much as he could from that experience. Around this time, Adam tried his first yoga class. He had reached the point where he would try anything, despite the fact that he was skeptical about yoga. The class was just for veterans, which was comfortable for Adam. When Adam talked about his first yoga class, he remembered that he was asleep within 15 minutes. That's when he knew he was in the right place. Not only that, but the teacher allowed Adam to sleep for thirty minutes. When the class was over, he felt rested for the first since coming home. For Adam, this was enough to bring him back for more.

For the bouts of overwhelming rage, Adam reported that, after the yoga class, he felt calm. The process of working on his anger continues for him, but he was able to have an experience in his body of feeling at ease that he was able to duplicate successfully with most yoga classes that he attended thereafter. In fact, he reported that, as a result of the yoga, he felt that he was able to get more out of his talk therapy.

Finally, Adam explained that his regular yoga class attendance allowed him to feel more rested and more in control of himself. The way he put it was that he was feeling "more like myself again," which for him involved a greater sense of competence and control. Adam decided to become a yoga teacher so he could share something that he found truly meaningful and successful with his fellow veterans.

Adam's story hits on several key themes of trauma-sensitive yoga. Adam was experiencing a disturbance in his biorhythms and his ability to self-regulate. The medication that was supposed to be treating his symptoms instead led him to feel disconnected from the present moment and to experience a loss of efficacy, or the feeling that he was in control of his own life. Yoga helped him to calm his arousal enough that he could sleep (right in class!). This became a self-regulatory practice that he could use—a tool in his toolbox to manage the traumatic stress symptoms he was facing. Unlike the medications, yoga was something that Adam was in control of. He was able to feel that he had more choices about how to deal with his symptoms, and he was able to take effective action (practice, practice, and more practice) to build up these skills. Eventually, Adam was able to use yoga to transform this traumatic experience by helping other veterans deal with the postwar reactions that they were having.

Yoga provides many opportunities for recreating these rhythms. The exploration of rhythm can take on very tangible forms such as these when we use breath and movement to explore a sense of flow and timing—both within ourselves and in relation to others. There are two types of rhythm that can be explored in a yoga class, in the therapy office, or otherwise in the therapeutic milieu. *Intrapersonal* rhythm involves matching one's own breath and movement. *Interpersonal* rhythm concerns moving in synchrony with the others in the group. In order to experience moving rhythmically with self and others, please consider the following two variations of the same exercise.

SUN BREATHS

Creating Intrapersonal Rhythms

Though we will present this exercise in one particular way, like most of the exercises we introduce, it can have many variations that you are welcome to explore as you like. When you are ready, please find a comfortable seat. If you like, bring your hands to the tops of your thighs or toward your knees, palms down. When you inhale, lift your hands a few inches; when you exhale, bring your palms back to your legs. Inhale lift, exhale release. Feel free to take a moment or two to investigate breathing and moving—finding and honoring your own rhythm.

Creating Interpersonal Rhythms

For this one you will need a partner. It can be a friend or family member. It can be a yoga teacher or a therapist: anyone with whom you feel comfortable enough to try sharing this brief exercise. You begin as above, but you may need to talk your partner through it if he or she is unfamiliar with the exercise. When you are ready, decide which one of you will set the pace. It may be interesting to take turns with this leadership role, but someone will need to set a pace. When you are ready, the leader can begin to talk through the process of inhaling and lifting hands, then exhaling and lowering them. In this version of the exercise, the focus of the practice is to synchronize breath and movement with each other. Feel free to continue with this for a minute or two, bringing the practice to an end when you are ready.

Students and teachers can experiment with discovering their own intrapersonal rhythms and with creating synchronous interpersonal rhythms by breathing and moving together. As survivors reconnect rhythmically with themselves and others, they are reconnecting to the world, recreating a sense of meaning in their lives.[8]

Another aspect of rhythm that is very important in the context of a trauma-sensitive yoga practice is the element of time. Many survivors experience a troubled relationship to time. We have already examined the idea that flashbacks can bring a person back to a time and place that no longer exists—can keep them orbiting around a traumatic event that occurred somewhere in the past. The experience of a triggered reaction or flashback can cause a disruption in one's sense of time and connection to the surrounding world. Dissociation can also cause people to "lose time," which is a phenomenon in which time passes without a person's conscious awareness. Dr. van der Kolk often talks about the trauma survivor as living outside of time, of being stuck in the replay of the trauma over and over again, to the point where it feels like it will never end. Yoga offers many opportunities to experience things beginning and ending. Postures begin, there is some time to experience the sensations and to experiment with small changes, and then the experience ends, and we move on to something else.

One core technique we use as trauma-sensitive yoga teachers to reestablish this sense of time is called the *countdown*. We will explain the countdown in more detail in chapter 7, but basically it involves the teacher counting backward, out loud, while a form is being practiced. For example, the teacher may invite students to investigate a form by saying, "If you like, experiment with breathing in this posture for 5, 4, 3, 2, 1, and then release. Now let's move on...." There is a clear sense of duration, and a very important end point that is unambiguous. This sense of the time-limited nature of the posture can help students to tolerate some discomfort or doubt about their ability to sustain engagement with a form. Trauma-sensitive yoga teachers can help their students reestablish a sense of duration and a feeling that things end, even if they are challenging yoga postures!

five

For Survivors

Developing a Trauma-Sensitive Yoga Practice

While developing our trauma-sensitive yoga programs, we have asked for ongoing feedback and suggestions from the survivors with whom we have worked. Through these conversations, we have identified a number of questions that survivors often have when they are considering whether to seek out trauma-sensitive yoga, and how to negotiate this process.

How do I know if I am ready to try trauma-sensitive yoga?

We suggest that you take some time to consider your readiness to try yoga, including how challenging this type of physical practice might be for you. Have you done anything physical in a while? How comfortable are you with your body? Do you anticipate challenges? It can't hurt to think things through a bit before stepping into that yoga room.

We recommend that you identify a support group or person that you can talk with about your experience, good or bad. If you are in therapy, this may be an important discussion between you and your therapist. At the Trauma Center, everyone in our yoga classes has his or her own individual therapist. If a particular class or situation is uncomfortable, students automatically have someone to talk to about their experience.

As we have discussed in this book, the average yoga class at a health club or yoga studio holds the possibility for many triggers: from unsolicited physical contact, to very close quarters, to language that relies on verbal instructions and demands rather than offers and invitations. To avoid some of these issues, you may want to look around to see if there is a trauma-sensitive yoga class being offered near you. You are the ultimate judge regarding experiences that seem safe and beneficial for you. Investigate as best you can. Feel free to ask questions of yoga teachers, especially if they are calling their classes trauma-sensitive. Such teachers should welcome questions, and their ability to respond appropriately may give you a good sense of what the class itself will be like.

When thinking about whether or not you are ready for a yoga class, please be willing to decide that the time is not right for you. If you conclude that the risk is just too high, that the potential for a triggering experience is just too great, then you have made an honest assessment based on your own understanding of where you are in the moment. There are options besides attending a public class. Maybe using this book or other at-home products (yoga CDs or DVDs) is the better way to go for now. Pacing is very important in trauma treatment. If a yoga class feels unmanageable right now, you may wish to spend some time developing skills for managing the emotions that sometimes emerge during a yoga practice, prior to jumping in to what can be a challenging physical and emotional experience for many people.

If you decide to go to a class, be aware that triggers will probably come up even under the best of circumstances. Part of your work is to recognize those triggers and to be able to respond appropriately. This is an example of where a therapeutic relationship can be very helpful. You and your therapist can spend some time considering possible triggers and how you might respond. This may be work that you can do alone, but try to spend some time considering what coping skills you might use if you are triggered in the class.

Two big concerns that have come up over the years for Trauma Center yoga students who have gone on to experiment with other yoga classes in the community are (1) can I leave a class if it becomes uncomfortable for any reason? and (2) can I ask a yoga teacher to not touch me?

Can I leave a class if it becomes uncomfortable for any reason?

Yes! It is important to emphasize that we unequivocally support your choice to leave a class for any reason, but especially if you feel uncomfortable in the room. This is not an endurance contest. We suggest that you build a yoga practice that is, on balance, comfortable and safe. This is not to say that it might not be very difficult and at times feel almost impossible. If you need to, feel free to leave the yoga class. Later, consider whether it was something about the class or the teacher, or if you just needed to leave as a way of managing emotions that were coming up in the moment. Let that reflection help you decide whether or not to return to that class again. If you live in a city, there are probably several classes for you to choose from. Feel free to shop around. Yoga can be a central part of your healing; or, if you push yourself too hard, it can become one more source of discomfort or distress. This is about taking care of yourself and beginning to reclaim your body, but it will probably be a long-term process. Please be patient and compassionate with yourself.

Can I ask a yoga teacher to not touch me?

Yes! It is entirely appropriate for you to approach a yoga teacher before the class starts and tell her or him that you do not want to be physically assisted during class. How the instructor responds will be informative. We urge all yoga instructors to agree to and support this request from students without hesitation or question. Yoga teachers should respect the wishes of their students above all else. The request for no physical assists does not impinge on a teacher's ability to lead a safe and effective class. Yoga teachers should be able to keep students safe without having to perform physical assists. Nevertheless, it is possible that a yoga teacher could be so set on a particular way of doing things that he or she may not be comfortable honoring your direction. It happens. For this reason, you may want to interview the teacher before taking a class, asking pertinent questions about the teacher's approach, including physical assists. In this sense, you are a consumer in a market, and you have the right to find the product that is best for you.

What guidance can you give on finding a trauma-sensitive yoga class?

There may be a class near you that calls itself "trauma-sensitive," and this may be a good place to start. Even if you are dealing with a public yoga studio or a gym setting, you may want to set up a time to meet the teacher before you take a class with him or her. Treat this like an interview where you get to ask questions about how the teacher handles the class and what kind of training he or she has had. Even five minutes should be enough time for you to get a sense about whether or not the class is worth a try. If a teacher is not willing to meet with you, this might be a signal that the class will not be trauma-sensitive. Trust your instincts. Be willing to be wrong. That is, you might hate the class once you try it, but at least you tried. Some survivors have expressed to us that they felt that they had "failed" in some way after having a negative experience in a yoga class. We encourage you, instead, to view the decision to discontinue an experience that is uncomfortable or distressing as a moment of self-care. You are making sure that you are protecting yourself and seeking out truly healing experiences. If you have a negative experience in one class or with one teacher or studio, do not be discouraged. Remember that there may be a class or teacher out there that is a better fit for you.

An At-Home Practice

Throughout this book we have offered individual yoga practices for you to experiment with. Now, we'd like to offer a full, sequential, mat-based practice. While the practice will be presented in a linear way and as something that can be done from beginning to end, you can approach it in different ways. You might choose to look the whole thing over and decide how you would like to approach it—do you want to try the whole sequence? Or would you rather experiment with one or two postures? The practice is intended to represent a very gentle, introductory class similar to one at the Trauma Center. But, in looking it through, you may decide that certain postures will not be helpful or interesting to you at this time. We encourage you to modify as you see fit. While, in general, you might expect the whole practice to take between thirty and forty-five minutes, the pacing will be up to you. Feel free to experiment with moving through the sequence more quickly, or with slowing down and bringing your full attention to each pose. We have provided pictures for those who are visual learners. It is our hope that if you so choose, you could skip the text and simply follow the pictures.

Getting Prepared

When you are ready, select a comfortable space for your practice. Make sure you have enough room to stretch out a little. A yoga mat may give you a good blueprint for the type of space you will need, but if you don't have a yoga mat, that's fine. Look for a comfortable spot of floor that is carpeted. If there is no carpet available, you may want a few towels nearby for padding at different points (we will indicate ideas for padding as they arise). Feel free to have some music if you like—any music! This is an experiment, and you may discover that listening to your favorite music is helpful. You may also want to experiment without music and see what you prefer. Consider what amount of time you have available for your yoga practice: is it a few minutes, or do you expect a full forty-five minutes without interruptions? You may want to shut off your phone, close down the computer, and do anything else that you can in order to give yourself a little time and space to simply focus on your yoga practice. If interruptions come, that's OK, but taking a few minutes to try to create for yourself a protected time and space may be worthwhile.

The Practice

The following postures are presented in this order:

Seated Mountain

Begin in a seated posture when you are ready. Give yourself a moment to experiment with a seated form that is comfortable enough for you. You may want to sit with your legs crossed. Another option is to sit back on your heels. Feel free to try something, and if that does not work, try something else. You can always change. You never have to remain stuck.

Once you have found a seated posture that works, you may wish to experiment with some gentle movements from your hips: rocking forward and back, side to side. You can also make these movements more circular, rounding out the edges. If you like, take a moment to move, getting a feeling for the space around you and a sense for your body in relation to that space (moving freely for twenty seconds to one minute).

Seated Mountain

When you are ready, beginning to move toward stillness. Movements become smaller and slower as you home in on stillness. This version of the Mountain posture is an upright, seated form. Once you are sitting upright, feel free to take a moment to experiment with sitting tall. We invite you to shift your awareness to the crown of your head, the very top of your head.

You may experiment with a gentle lifting of your torso, a gentle lengthening through the very top of your head, allowing your spine to be naturally tall. This does not have to be an aggressive action; you are simply allowing your spine to be naturally tall and upright. Notice the source in your body of this shift in posture. Which muscles are engaged in your lengthening, and which muscles remain at ease? This is an investigation that you may wish to return to many times throughout your practice: cultivating a dual awareness of which muscles you are engaging in a posture and which you can let go.

Seated Mountain

Seated Noticing Breath

As you are ready, begin to notice your breath. For the purpose of this exercise the suggestion is simply to notice that you are breathing. You may be breathing through your nose or mouth. Just notice. As you move through this yoga practice, you may want to experiment with breathing through your nose or mouth and discover what feels right to you. The sole goal of this exercise is to become more aware of what feels most comfortable and natural to you in terms of breathing.

Seated Sun Breaths

VARIATION A: Now consider, if you like, experimenting with some breathing and moving in unison. With your hands on your thighs or toward your knees, as you inhale, gently lift your hands a few inches. Then, as you exhale, bring your hands back to your thighs or knees. Inhale lift, exhale gently release.

Sun Breath with hands gently lifted on inhalation

Feel free to breathe and move here for a few cycles, getting a sense for connecting your breath and your movement. If you want to add something, spread your fingers wide apart on the in-breath, making your hands very active, broad and firm. With your out-breath, soften your hands as completely as possible, like feathers floating down to rest on your thighs or knees. Notice the contrast between activating and softening your hands.

Sun Breath with palms together in front of the heart

VARIATION B: Another Sun Breath variation is to begin with your palms together in front of your heart.

Sun Breath with arms extended to the sides upon inhalation

As you inhale, extend your arms to your sides.

As you exhale, bring your palms back together in front of your heart. Feel free to continue with this pattern for a few cycles. Notice that this is a bigger gesture. What does it feel like to take up a little more space?

VARIATION C: If you would like to experiment with a yet more spacious variation, begin as in Variation A with your hands on your thighs or knees. As you inhale, sweep your arms high in a big circle.

Sun Breath with arms sweeping high upon inhalation

When you exhale, bring your hands back to your thighs or knees. Notice that this variation is more circular, while the other two are more linear. Notice what it feels like to explore a more spacious gesture like this. *You can always return to Variation A or B at any point. In fact, attending to your body and noticing what is and is not comfortable and making choices according to these observations is at the heart of this practice.* Feel free to take another minute or two to explore your Sun Breaths.

Seated Neck Rolls

When you are ready, we invite you to return to your upright, seated pose. Now, relaxing the muscles of your neck, allow your chin to droop gently toward your heart, your sternum.

Neck Roll with gentle lowering of the chin

Next, gently roll your left ear toward your left shoulder.

Slowly roll your head from side to side a few times, gently dropping your chin through the middle. Allow yourself to move and breathe freely. Begin to get a feeling for some of the muscles of your neck and upper back. With this movement, explore the bottom half of a circle or sphere. You may notice a lot of sensation here. These are muscles that can be very tight for many of us. If it is painful, you can always stop. You always have that control. Another option might be to make the movements smaller. See if that enables you to keep moving but without any pain. Or, you may wish to experiment with making the movements bigger if there is no discomfort. Feel free to take a moment to explore these neck rolls. When you are ready, gently guide your chin back to your center, toward your heart, and then lift it upward to its normal orientation.

Neck Roll toward left shoulder

Seated Shoulder Circles

VARIATION A: If you like, begin to make some gentle circles with your shoulders, starting in one direction.

Shoulder Circle variation with elbows

You can make these circles very small, or you can make them big—that is up to you. You have total control over the size of the circles you are making with your shoulders. As you like, feel free to reverse the direction a few times. Notice how you are beginning to get a feeling for your shoulders: how they move and the space around them. If you like, continue this exploration of your shoulders for a moment.

VARIATION B: Another option is to bring your fingertips to the tops of your shoulders and experiment with using the tips of your elbows to draw circles.

Now you are adding another dimension to this exercise, exploring the space *across* your chest and collarbones and the space *across* your upper back. Feel free to reverse direction a few times. When you are ready, if you like, pause and shake it out through your fingers. Gently shake it out from your shoulders through your fingertips.

Table

For this posture, if you do not have a mat or a carpeted floor, you may want to use towels underneath you in a way that makes you more comfortable.

As you are ready, come into your Table—that's knees under hips and wrists under shoulders.

In this form you may notice muscles in your arms beginning to engage. If you like, you can gently shift around, emphasizing the weight on your hands and your knees, getting a feeling for some muscles in your arms starting to wake up. Other musculature that you may notice is that of the lower abdomen, or core. You may choose to experiment with hugging your lower belly in gently as a way of interacting with some muscles right at your center. These core muscles can become a great resource, and we will check in with them periodically throughout the practice.

Table pose with hands to the floor and knees under hips

Child's Pose

For this posture, if you do not have a mat or a carpeted floor, you may want to use towels underneath your knees in a way that makes you more comfortable. To transition from Table to Child's Pose, bring your big toes together and begin to experiment with sitting back toward your heels. With your big toes together and sitting back toward your heels, next consider some of the options described below.

For some it may be most comfortable to have knees together.

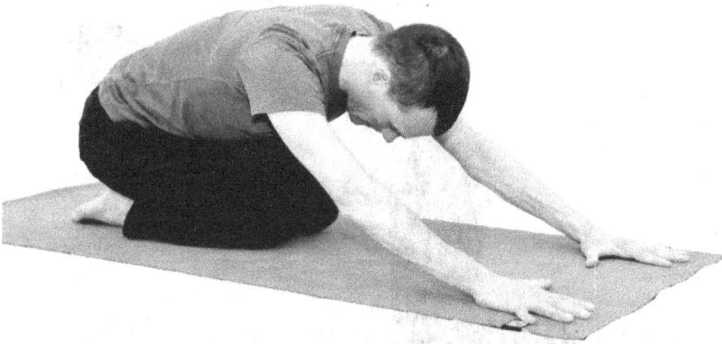

Child's Pose with knees together

For others, knees may be slightly wider than hips.

In either case, once you find a comfortable variation for yourself, if you like, extend your arms forward.

Another option is to stack your fists and rest your forehead on top of your fists.

Child's Pose with knees wider than hips

Child's Pose with arms extended forward

Child's Pose with forehead resting on top of fists

When you have found the variation of this pose that feels most comfortable to you, investigate lengthening your back through your tailbone. Cultivate some length in your lower back. Experience taking care of your lower back through this exercise. Feel free to give yourself a moment to breathe comfortably here.

Child's Pose Side Stretch

When you are ready, if you like, walk your hands slightly over to your left side, shifting your whole upper body slightly to your left for a side stretch.

Notice the side stretch, and feel free to give yourself a moment to breathe with it, taking care of the side of your body as you breathe. After a few breaths, feel free to switch sides, walking your hands around to your right. Notice that you have control over how much you are shifting. It may be that a slight shift works best, or you can make it more pronounced. That is up to you. Give yourself a moment to breathe with the side stretch on both sides. When you are ready, come back to the middle. Find the middle for yourself.

Child's Pose Side Stretch, shifting upper body to the right

Cat Tilts

For this posture, if you do not have a mat or a carpeted floor, you may want to use towels underneath you in a way that makes you more comfortable.

From Child's Pose move back to Table. If you like, from Table, as you inhale, gently lift your tailbone and your chin.

Next, as you exhale, gently round your spine.

As you inhale, gently lift; as you exhale, gently round. Feel free to continue for a moment at your own pace. This is an opportunity to find your own rhythm, to honor your own rhythm. If you like, you can experiment with going fast or slow. Perhaps through experimenting you will get a sense for what feels natural to you in the moment. If you like, take a moment for this experiment. When you are ready, exhale yourself back to Table, back to neutral.

Cat Tilt, gently lifting chin and tailbone upon inhalation

Cat Tilt, gently rounding spine upon exhalation

Standing Mountain

From Table, as you are ready, walk up to a standing position. Give yourself a moment to get a feeling for standing. If you like, rest your arms at your sides, and set your feet about hip's width apart and parallel to each other.

Standing Mountain

You may engage in this exercise with your eyes open or closed; that is up to you. If open, you may want to glance down toward the floor at a comfortable angle. As best you can, notice your feet on the ground. Shift your attention to your feet and observe what you notice. Maybe there are some things you can do in order to cultivate some feeling for your feet being on the ground, like tapping your heels or tapping your toes. If it is helpful, feel free to look down at your feet as a way of noticing that your feet are on the ground. Take a moment for this investigation if you like.

Next, with your feet on the ground, shift your awareness to the crown of your head, the very top of your head. Maybe gently lift through the top of your head as a way of interacting with standing up tall. What does that feel like? If you like, give yourself a moment to notice where it comes from in your body when you lift up gently through the top of your head.

Finally, with your feet on the ground and standing up naturally tall, bring your awareness to your center. If it is helpful, experiment with gently hugging in around and just below your navel. As you gently draw in around your lower belly, begin to recognize your center as a source of strength and support. This muscular action does not have to be aggressive. Muscular energy in this yoga practice is supportive energy. It is stabilizing. It is intentional and purposeful. If you like, give yourself a moment to experience your center as a source of intention and purpose.

Tree

When you are ready, bring your palms together in front of your heart and begin to shift your weight over onto your right leg. If you like, you can keep your left toes gently on the floor.

Another option is to turn your left knee out and gently tuck your left foot into your right ankle.

Another option is to bring your foot just above your ankle.

Feel free to take a moment to experiment with this aspect of the form.

Another aspect of the form to experiment with is your arms. You can keep your palms together in front of your heart, or you can extend your arms to the sides.

Alternately, you may wish to sweep your arms up overhead and see what that is like for you.

Tree pose with left toes gently on the floor

Tree pose with left foot tucked in gently to right ankle

Tree pose with foot just above ankle

In any case, feel free to take a moment to investigate all of these different options available in the form. You may even come up with some of your own.

Two other things to consider are your *gaze* and your *breath*.

GAZE IN TREE. For some of us it may be helpful to pick one point on the wall or floor and to focus our gaze on that one point. You can also experiment by looking at your fingertips or even closing your eyes. Notice if these different options change your experience in the form. This is a nonjudgmental experimenting. If something does not work or becomes uncomfortable for any reason, you can always change. Underlying this yoga practice is a commitment to taking care of ourselves, and the encouragement is to not do anything in this yoga practice that causes you pain or discomfort.

Tree pose with arms extended to sides

Tree pose with arms extended overhead

BREATH IN TREE. In general with this yoga practice, breathing should be free and easy. The Tree form may be an opportunity for you to check in on your breath and see what's happening. Notice if you are holding your breath, or breathing in any way that does not feel free and easy. If you can, see if you can interact with your breath a little and encourage it to be free and easy. If you notice that your breath is really uncomfortable in this or any form, the encouragement is to stop what you are doing, return to a comfortable, neutral position, and see if you can find a different form that allows you to breathe comfortably.

When you are ready, feel free to experiment with Tree on your other leg.

Chair

Returning to the Standing Mountain posture, as you are ready, soften your knees as if you are just about to sit down into a chair. Next, extend and sweep your arms up by your ears.

Chair pose with arms extended

Chair pose with arms to sides

How deeply you sit into your hips is up to you, but the encouragement is to be cautious and take it slow. This is a very intense, very muscular form. As you sit into your hips, you may wish to experiment with hugging your lower belly in and interacting with that strength and stability at your center. This core strength will support your lower back. If your shoulders become uncomfortable at all, another option is to bring your arms to your sides.

In either case, experiment with drawing your shoulders back and hugging your shoulder blades in toward the midline of your back. You may feel some muscles really engaging around and between your shoulder blades. As you tone and brighten these muscles between your shoulder blades, your neck may be able to release a little bit. If you like, you can experiment with lengthening your neck gently by drawing your shoulder blades gently down your back and away from your ears. Feel free to take a moment to notice and interact with your core strength and your leg strength, breathing free and easy. Investigate strength and breath in the Chair pose. Other names for this posture are Thunderbolt and Fierce Pose. When you are ready, slowly come back to your Standing Mountain form.

Standing Forward Fold

From Standing Mountain, as you are ready, slowly begin to fold forward. One option is to bring your forearms to your thighs or toward your knees, like a crouch. Another option is to allow your hands to be free, fingertips gently reaching toward the floor (it is fine if your fingertips do not touch the floor).

Or, if you like, take the opposite hand to the opposite elbow.

Standing Forward Fold with hands free

In any case, the suggestion is to keep your knees slightly bent. Notice how you are standing. If most of your weight is back on your heels, notice what happens if you shift some weight forward, just behind your toes. Does that shift have an effect on the Forward Fold dynamic? If you like, feel free to shake your head "yes" and "no," inviting gravity into your neck and shoulders. With some gentle movements you may enhance your interaction with gravity—allowing gravity to have an effect in the big muscles around your neck and upper back, lower back, maybe even around your spine itself. Feel free to hang out here for half a minute or so, breathing free and easy. When you are ready, slowly begin to roll up to a standing position. If you feel any discomfort in your lower back you can support yourself with your hands on your legs as you make your way up to standing. Another suggestion is to take it extra slow, especially if you get dizzy at all. Take your time as you unfurl back into your Standing Mountain posture. Once you are upright, feel free to give yourself a moment to stand, simply standing and breathing. Allow yourself a moment to interact with standing. Another invitation might be to give yourself a moment to stand as you would like to stand. Allow your breath and posture some space to evolve to where you feel as present, as upright, as strong, and as at ease as you would like.

Standing Forward Fold with opposite hand to opposite elbow

Shoulder Down Bridge

For this posture, if you do not have a mat or a carpeted floor, you may want to use towels underneath you in a way that makes you more comfortable.

For this posture, as you are ready, end up lying down, arms at your sides and feet flat on the floor about a hip's width apart and parallel.

If you like, take a moment to experiment with this alignment. Begin to get a feeling for your feet on the ground and a sense for what hip width and parallel are for you. It does not have to be perfect. Next, when you are ready, press down through your feet to lift your hips.

Preparation for Bridge pose

Bridge pose, gently pressing down through both feet to lift hips

Perhaps you lift your hips a fraction of an inch from the floor. Maybe you experiment with lifting your hips a few inches from the floor. It does not matter how high you lift your hips. This is an experiment. There is no one posture we are trying to achieve. The suggestion is to really tune into your body, your experience. If you notice that something is uncomfortable for any reason, please be willing to come out of the form, to change what you are doing in order to make yourself more comfortable. You always have this control and this practice of listening to your body and making choices according to what you discover is right for you at this moment in your practice. Make sure you can breathe freely, that your lower back and your knees are comfortable. Give yourself a moment.

ADDING SOMETHING. If you would like to add something here, the suggestion is to turn your palms up toward the sky. When you do this, you will rotate your upper arm bones in their sockets in a way that makes it easier for you to tuck your shoulders a little closer together underneath you. Take a moment to walk your shoulders a little closer together underneath your body. As you do this, you will be hugging your shoulder blades more firmly onto your back. You may feel some muscles begin to engage around and between your shoulder blades. These are key muscles for stability in your upper body. Your feet press to lift your hips, but it is your shoulders that press down to lift up your heart a little. Over time, your whole spine may be off the floor, with no direct pressure on the vertebrae whatsoever. Feel free to take a moment bringing your shoulders underneath you and feeling that support, strength, and stability in your upper body.

KEY LEG MUSCLES. Here is one more detail if you would like to experiment further. We have started to identify the muscles around and between your shoulder blades as key muscles for support and stability in your upper body. Similarly, there are key muscles for support and stability in your lower body. Particularly in the Bridge pose, you can investigate your inner thigh muscles. If you bring your knees a little bit closer toward each other, with a slight shift toward the midline, you may notice your inner thigh muscles begin to engage. Inner thigh muscles may begin to brighten and activate. Inner thigh muscles support your lower back and stabilize your knees. They are key muscles for balance and stability.

If you like, take a moment to interact with, investigate, and claim your inner thigh muscles. Meanwhile, continue to breathe free and easy through your nose or your mouth. When you are ready, slowly lower your hips and bring your sacrum (just below your lower back) down to the floor.

Full Body Extension

If you like, stretch out your legs comfortably in front of you.

This may be enough for now, but feel free to extend your arms up over your head so you are pointing your fingertips behind you.

You do not have to point straight back; there are many angles here for you to explore. Especially if you feel any pinching or tightness in your lower back, you may wish to bring your arms to your sides and see if that takes the strain out of your back.

Full Body Extension with legs extended

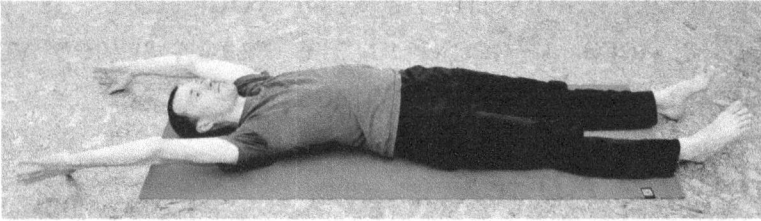

Full Body Extension, legs and arms extended

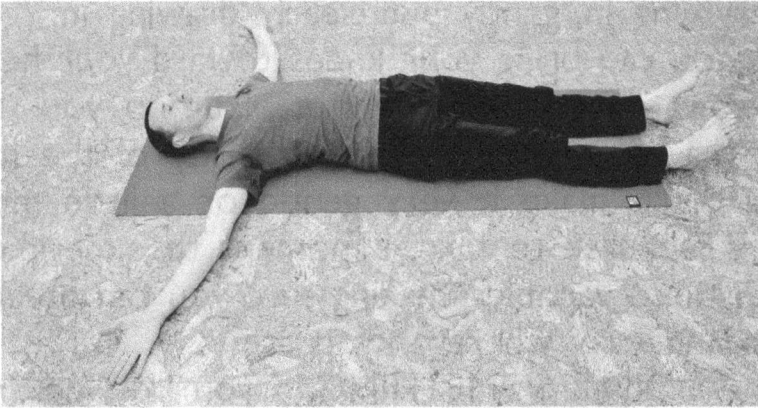

Full Body Extension, legs extended and arms to sides

Extending your arms overhead to some degree may be more abdominal, more muscular. If it is helpful, hug your lower belly in a bit to notice and cultivate strength right at your core. Feel free to investigate being long. One way to get a little longer is to move your fingers and toes and experiment with lengthening through the tips of your fingers and toes, through the *spaces between* your fingers and toes. Feel free to take a moment, breathing freely, to experiment with being long. Perhaps you will even sense a connection between the tips of your fingers and the tips of your toes as you breathe here. When you are ready, sweep your arms up and hug your knees in.

Hugging Knees

This posture is a companion to the Full Body Extension. Now, the experiment is hugging everything in, gently but clearly drawing in.

You can bring your knees toward your heart or toward your shoulders; it is up to you. You also have control over the intensity of the hug. You could make it very gentle or a little more firm. Feel free to take a moment to experiment with these variables, making sure you can breathe free and easy wherever you are.

ADDING SOMETHING. If you like, feel free to move, gently rocking your knees to one side and your chin to the other. This movement can be tiny, or you can make it more pronounced. If moving becomes uncomfortable for any reason, you can always stop and breathe in a neutral form. If you like, feel free to explore this form for a moment. When you are ready, roll onto one side and gently press up into a seated position.

Hugging Knees

Boat

As you begin to experience your core as a source of stability and support, it may be interesting to take a moment to focus on core strength and power. From a seated form, bring your feet flat onto the floor. You have several options with your hands. Here are three: You can place your hands a few inches behind your hips.

Another option is to bring your hands to your shins.

And a third option is to bring your arms to your sides, palms facing each other.

Boat pose with hands behind and on the floor

Boat pose with hands to shins

Boat pose with arms to sides and palms facing each other

Notice the space between your thighs and your upper body. It may be interesting to recline slightly. Lean back just a little bit from where you are, catching yourself with your center, your lower belly muscles. You might find it helpful to experiment with hugging or drawing in your lower belly as a way of interacting with your core strength. Meanwhile, continue breathing free and easy. In fact, you may even want to experiment with *adding a little breath:* basically just adding a little depth to your inhale and exhale. See what it feels like to breathe a little deeper than normal in this form. Does your breath have an effect on your experience in this form? Does your breathing support your form in any way? Does your breathing soothe or soften your effort, affording you some ease in the midst of this muscular effort? Feel free to take a moment to explore the form of your Boat pose.

When you are ready, bring your hands behind you and lift your feet off the floor. This may be more muscular, and the suggestion is to take it slow; but if you like, when you are ready, bring your hands to the floor behind you and extend your legs forward. You can hold this form and breathe free and easy for three to five breaths.

Make sure you can breathe comfortably. *Sometimes we can force ourselves into postures, and we end up holding our breath.* Check it out for yourself and see if you are able to breathe comfortably. The suggestion is to prioritize your breath and back down from a posture or a variation of a posture in order to be able to breathe freely.

Boat pose, hands to the floor behind and legs extended

Seated Forward Fold/Hip Stretch

Beginning with both legs extended forward, when you are ready, gently bend one leg.

If you like, you can place a yoga block, blanket, pillow, or some towels under the knee of your bent leg for support.

Using support under your knee is optional and may be something for you to experiment with. You may find that it is more comfortable for you without any support under the knee of your bent leg. Feel free to take a moment to investigate.

When you are ready, consider some further options with this form. For some of us it may be more comfortable to bring the hands a few inches behind the hips and lean back a little bit. For some of us it may feel best to sit up in the middle.

Seated Forward Fold, gently bending one leg

Seated Forward Fold with prop used for support

For some of us it may feel good to lengthen forward to some degree.

Seated Forward Fold, sitting up in the middle

Seated Forward Fold, lengthening forward

Seated Forward Fold, lengthening further

One suggestion if you are leaning forward is to soften and slightly bend the knee of that straight leg in order to avoid any undue strain on the joint. It does not matter how far you fold forward. As an experiment, you may want to see what it feels like to lead with your heart—let your heart come forward first so you are staying tall in the form. There are at least two ways to fold forward in this form. One is by rounding and basically collapsing into the front of your body. Another is by lengthening—staying "tall," leading with your heart.

While the suggestion in this book is to tend toward the lengthening variation, this may be a good chance for you to experiment for yourself. Be gentle, but feel free to try both variations and see what feels right to you. "Right" or "wrong," in the context of this yoga practice, does not have to be a moral issue; one variation of the form does not have more moral merit than another. They are simply options for you to explore and decide upon for yourself. If you conclude that rounding your back feels better, that is fine. It is OK to trust your body in that way.

Some further investigations of this posture might be to explore whether you can continue to breathe comfortably while rounding your back. Is there a point where your breath becomes uncomfortable or constricted at all? This form may be an opportunity for you to begin to investigate what makes sense to you, what feels right in your body. As you experiment and learn to listen to your body, the encouragement in this book will be to make the compassionate choice for yourself. If rounding your back a little feels better, that would be the compassionate choice. This may change over time. You may discover after some period of practice that lengthening the front of your body feels better, and then that becomes the compassionate choice. The goal of this book is to encourage you to make compassionate choices for yourself based right in your body rather than to prescribe one strict way to approach these forms. Feel free to give yourself a moment with this practice, breathing free and easy. When you are ready, switch sides and repeat this exercise. Once you have experimented with both sides, feel free to return to a comfortable seated posture.

Seated Forward Fold, rounding forward

Reclining Twist

When you are ready, begin by lying down with your feet flat on the floor about a hip's width apart and your arms to your sides like wings.

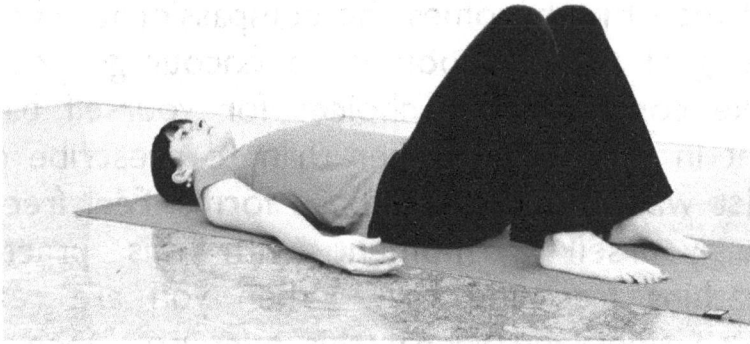

Preparation for Reclining Twist

Preparation for Reclining Twist, gently dropping both knees to one side

At your own pace, gently drop both knees comfortably to one side. Feel free to pause here and breathe for a moment. See if you can keep both shoulders on the ground. Notice the stability across your upper back with both shoulders comfortably but clearly rooted down to the floor. In a sense, your twist can show up as a result of this stability and safety around both shoulders. After a few breaths on one side, feel free to try the other side. You may wish to try both sides more than once. Give yourself a moment to explore breathing with this twist around your spine. When you are ready, come back to neutral, with both feet flat on the floor.

Final Resting Form

When you are ready, begin to find a form where you can rest for a moment. This may be arms and legs comfortably extended.

You could also cross your arms if that is more comfortable.

Actually, it could be any posture that is comfortable for you, including lying on one side or sitting up. Take a moment to experiment with different options. Feel free to have your eyes open or closed.

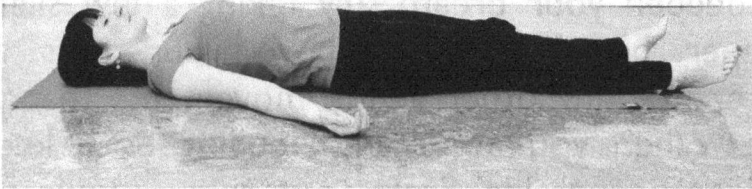

Final Resting Form with arms and legs comfortably extended

Final Resting Form with legs extended and arms crossed

If you have an alarm clock, you may want to set it for one minute when you are ready. The idea with the alarm clock is to give you a sense of what one minute is. You can always try other time increments, but do not feel like this has to be a long extended period. Mainly, you are giving yourself a little space. A moment in which you can simply *be*. A moment in which you do not have to explain yourself to anyone. A moment in which you do not have to make anything special happen. You are totally awake and completely present, but there is no need to make anything happen. Claim this moment of rest that belongs solely to you.

Finishing Your Practice

After a minute or so, if you like, gently begin to deepen your breath. Try taking a few slightly deeper breaths. Slowly move your toes and fingers, or any other gentle movements that you like. When you are ready, bending both knees, roll onto one side. From your side, at your own pace, move into an upright seated form. You may wish to use both hands to help you transition. Honoring your own rhythm as you move, end up in a seated form. Once you are sitting upright, feel free to pause. If you notice any tightness, any tension remaining in your body, you may be aware of some ways that you can move in order to invite that tension to release. Notice how it is possible to listen to your body in this way. Finally, when you are ready, slowly open your eyes if they are closed. Look around. Notice where you are. Notice how you feel in your body. May you benefit from your intention toward health and well-being that brought you to your yoga practice today.

six

For Clinicians

Integrating Yoga-Based Strategies into the Therapy Office

The clients I have been working with have literally expressed a readiness to "use their body" in a healing way. Through therapy they have developed a stronger sense of self, ego, and insight that has enabled many of them to progress toward understanding the mind-body connection.

THERAPIST integrating yoga-based interventions into therapeutic work

Supporting a client who has experienced any trauma over the course of their lifetime in simply noticing that they have a body, befriending their body, and incorporating exercises to develop healthy relationships with their body into therapy is integral to the treatment of trauma as the body can "hold" the trauma. I have found that, when introduced in a safe and comfortable space, clients tend to be willing and able to acknowledge and nurture the mind-body connection. As a clinician, it can be a very rewarding and exciting experience to be present with a client who is ready to and engages in taking care of the body as well as the mind following experiences with trauma.

THERAPIST integrating yoga-based interventions into therapeutic work

There are a number of ways that yoga-based practices may be incorporated into the therapy process. While these themes may be helpful to yoga practitioners or teachers (some material will be familiar from other sections of this book), we hope that this section will provide therapists with a framework for conceptualizing why and how to incorporate trauma-sensitive yoga into their therapy practice.

Integrating yoga-based practices into therapy is a very fluid and adaptable process, with many different options. For instance, you and your client may decide together to focus on one exercise and to incorporate it into several sessions in a row, or you may decide to experiment with trying several different exercises. You may decide to open and close each session with a yoga-based practice, or you may integrate yoga-based strategies into the session as a means of practicing self-awareness or affect regulation. Despite this flexibility, there are a number of general "best practices" in terms of integrating yoga into therapy. Before you get started, we would like to offer several recommendations for introducing yoga-based interventions into the therapy office:

- It is generally helpful for the facilitator to have a personal experience of yoga practice. Attending yoga classes or using videos to guide an at-home yoga practice will give you a firsthand experience of the internal states that you will be focusing on with your clients. It will also likely help you to understand some of the anxieties that yoga practitioners may experience as they are learning a yoga practice, as well as some of the pitfalls that yoga instructors may encounter.

- We suggest that you read the exercises first before presenting them to someone else. Even better, pick some and practice them yourself. Then try facilitating these exercises with your colleagues, family, and friends. Get as much practice as you can to increase your own comfort with these exercises. Use the scripts provided, and say the words out loud. You will probably want to make some changes in the language so that it feels more natural to you. Feel free to modify in this way.

- You, the facilitator, will need to develop your own "yoga voice," which includes finding a pace of delivery and vocal quality that are calming. In general, we suggest a slow, methodical delivery in which your voice is soft and gentle, but clear. We invite you to treat each period in the script as a chance for you to pause and take one to three free and easy breaths. Eventually set your instructional rhythm according to your most comfortable, relaxed breathing pattern.

- When facilitating the exercises, we suggest that you participate along with your clients. By practicing together, you can get feedback through your own actual experience, so the endeavor becomes less theoretical and more concrete and visceral. Rather than a prescriptive approach ("you try this, while I observe the outcome"), yoga can become a shared experience that may strengthen the bond between therapist and client. Pay attention to "staying with" the client and guiding them slowly to shift how they are approaching the exercise. For instance, if your client is engaging in a breathing exercise with rapid, shallow breaths, match him or her and then gently guide your client in slowing the pace and engaging in fuller breaths. For a teaching technique, you may benefit from referring to "The Countdown," in chapter 7, which is dedicated to core elements of trauma-informed yoga instruction.

- After engaging your client in yoga exercises, we suggest that you spend some time debriefing the experience so that the yoga becomes an integrated part of the therapy process. Some yogabased practices may bring up material that should be addressed clinically. For instance, a client may experience triggered emotions or memories when using yoga-based interventions. Your individual clients are likely to provide you with important feedback that will help make these exercises more beneficial. Please be willing to listen and to respond using all of your therapeutic training and instincts.

- Clients may find particular exercises that they can take with them out of the office that can become resources in their daily life. You may wish to encourage them to practice these exercises between sessions to consolidate learning.

The therapist's own self-awareness and self-care are important components of any type of therapy. This includes knowing when you need to take a few minutes to stretch or take a break in between sessions. It includes being aware of the number of clients that you take on, the emotional impact of the work that you are doing, and the need to seek supervision or consultation. It is particularly important when doing body-based therapy that the therapist's self-awareness encompasses the somatic realm, as well as the cognitive and emotional realms. That is, have you built up muscular tension throughout your day? Are you exhausted? Are you feeling disconnected from your body? Before we get started thinking about the types of interventions we might use in the therapy office, take a few minutes to check in about how you are doing and to connect with yourself somatically. This is a type of practice that you might implement in between clients to make sure that you are fully present and self-aware.

SHOULDER ROLLS FOR SELF-AWARENESS AND TENSION RELEASE

If you wish, pause for a moment from your reading. The intention for these exercises is to find what works for you whether you are sitting, standing, or lying down. Please take a moment to find an orientation that works for you. Whether you are standing or sitting, take a moment to interact with the space around you. Maybe some very gentle movements will help. Maybe these movements are barely perceptible; maybe they are bigger. Begin to get a sense of the space around you and of your body in relation to that space. Feel free to give yourself a moment here. When you are ready, move toward stillness. At your own pace, begin to make circles with your shoulders. Starting in one direction, begin to get a feeling for some space around your shoulders. These circles can be tiny, barely perceptible. They may also be bigger. In any case, give yourself a moment to explore the way that your shoulders can move. Feel free to reverse the direction of the circles a few times if you like. Your breath is free and easy, as are your movements. Feel free to stay with this one, or you can add something if you like: bring your fingertips to the tops of your shoulders. Now, begin to draw circles with the tips of your elbows. This engages some other muscles that run from your sternum and your collarbones out to the tips of your shoulders—the head of the arm bones. Feel free to give yourself a moment to experiment with some movement here. When you are ready, gently come back toward stillness, toward neutral, and enjoy a few breaths.

Matching Yoga-Based Interventions to Goals

The specific yoga postures that are chosen can be selected on the basis of one's unique challenges and goals. The table in section entitled "Matching Yoga-Based Interventions to Goals" provides some examples of chair-based yoga postures that could be selected for use within a therapy context or for use at home. Each posture is linked to a unique challenge and goal. This table is not comprehensive, and it is meant as a series of examples. Different people will resonate with different postures for each general goal. The challenge is to determine the unique postures, breathing exercises, and practice guidelines that work for each person!

In the coming sections, we will explore a number of common goals in trauma treatment. We will link each of these goals with examples of yoga-based exercises that can be used to address that specific goal. Some of these goals include creating present-moment focus; developing mindfulness skills; building curiosity and developing tolerance for experiencing sensation; changing one's relationship to one's body; centering; grounding; building affect-regulation skills; practicing choice; integrating aspects of experience; increasing confidence; and building connection to others.

Note: Most of these exercises are chair based. You will need to consider the orientation of the chairs. If there are two people in the space together, the suggestion is that you position the chairs so that you are not facing each other head on. If either of you decide to keep your eyes open, it may become uncomfortable to be looking directly at the face or the body of the other person. We suggest that you find a way to position the chairs so that each person could keep their eyes open and be looking at a neutral space in the room (such as the floor or a wall).

MATCHING YOGA-BASED STRATEGIES TO GOALS FOR INTERVENTION

Challenge	Goal	Chair-based Yoga Posture
Feeling frozen, rigid, holding on to things (hoarding, constipation)	Letting go	Forward Fold
Anxiety, tension, panic	Decreasing hyperarousal	Neck Rolls, Ratio Breathing, Belly Breathing
Isolation	Building relationship	Mirrored mindful integrated movement; group practice
Defensiveness, avoidance of intimacy	Opening boundaries	Sun Breaths
Dissociation	Grounding	Mountain pose, noticing feet on floor
Feeling off-balance, conflicting feelings	Centering	Seated Twist, Seated Triangle, Seated Eagle, balanced movement, bringing awareness to core
Emotionally overwhelmed, unprotected	Containment	Child's pose (adapted)
Stuck, unable to make decisions or take action, unable to defend self	Unfreezing; reorganizing active defenses	Movement-based postures
Somatic dissociation, emotional numbing	Awareness of body	Any mindfulness practice
Reenactments, revictimization	Boundaries	Sensing body, creating physical boundaries
Feeling helpless, disempowered	Empowerment (feeling core power)	Lengthening spine, Leg lifts, moving to standing posture
Emotionally numb or shut down, low energy	Decreasing hypoarousal	Activating postures (standing), breathwork

Creating Present-Moment Focus

> It has felt harder to be present in the last two classes ... or maybe I am just noticing that I am not present more often.
> YOGA STUDENT at the Trauma Center

Many trauma survivors develop a heightened sense of fear and anxiety about the future. They may also be frequently triggered, which brings them back into the past. The present focus of yoga encourages living in the moment. Consider experimenting with the following exercise as a way of creating a present-moment focus. It is possible to talk with clients about the idea of living in the here and now. It is possible to strategize with them about ways for them to practice being in the here and now. But ultimately, if you are just talking, it is all theoretical. We are suggesting that, with trauma survivors, focusing solely on theory and using talk may not be sufficient. Let's practice being in the present moment, right here, right now.

LIVING IN THE PRESENT—NOTICING YOUR FEET ON THE GROUND

If you like, feel free to take off your shoes (this may allow a more organic experience with the exercise). As you are ready, bring your feet flat onto the floor. As best you can, feel your feet making contact with the floor. Maybe there are some things you can do that help you notice your feet on the ground. You may experiment with tapping your heels. You may experiment with moving your toes. Feel free to take a moment to get a feeling for your feet on the ground. The sensation may come in flickers. The encouragement is to stay with those flickers and notice them; experiment with those moments when you notice your feet on the ground. It may be specific parts of your foot that you notice touching the floor. Pause for a few breaths as you experiment with noticing your feet making contact with the floor.

Please note that this exercise may be done seated or standing. If standing, you can also experiment with feeling your feet on the floor—noticing your feet and the floor interacting to support your standing.

Developing Mindfulness Skills

Yoga also encourages an increased awareness of the self, including thoughts, feelings, and somatic reactions. This increase in interoceptive awareness helps people to rebuild a connection with their bodies and with their sense of self. With trauma-sensitive yoga, we have found that mindfulness[1] practices are more successful when they are very clearly directed and also body oriented. Rather than ask people to be aware of their thoughts or feelings, or even the sights, sounds, and smells in their environment, we are suggesting something like the following.

DEVELOPING MINDFULNESS—NASAL BREATHING

Please note: It has been our subjective experience that many of our clients tend to breathe with their mouths and, prominently, with the secondary breathing muscles. See the section entitled "Breathing Practices and Affect Regulation" for more information on breathing practices.

When you are ready, begin to notice your breath. You may have your eyes open or closed; that is up to you. If you like, you may experiment with breathing in and out through your nose. For some of us who are used to breathing with our mouth, nasal breathing may be a practice. If you decide to experiment with nasal breathing, please know that if it becomes uncomfortable for any reason, you can always breathe through your mouth. Pause for a moment to try breathing through your nose for a few cycles and then, if you like, shift to breathing through your mouth. Do you notice any differences? Do you notice that one is more comfortable for you than the other? If so, just notice. If not, that is fine. When you are ready, come back to your natural breath.

If you are introducing this exercise in the therapy office, you might wish to process what this experience was like. You can notice together any signs of discomfort or self-judgment, and then return to the exercise again, working to create a curious and nonjudgmental stance to all aspects of the experience.

Building Curiosity and Developing Tolerance for Experiencing Sensation

One of the important facets of "distress tolerance"[2]—building up our capacity to manage uncomfortable physical and emotional states—is moving away from judgment of these states. Curiosity helps to create emotional distance in which people are able to "just notice" their internal states, without taking immediate action to try to shift these states. Trauma-sensitive yoga offers specific practices that encourage a nonjudgmental, dispassionate curiosity without the need to change anything.

One way we do this is in our use of *language of inquiry*, using words like "notice," "investigate," "experiment," and "curious." In the context of individual psychotherapy, one important element of developing tolerance for experiencing sensation is to cultivate identification, labeling, and communication of internal states and sensations that may arise in a yoga practice. Creating a language about our internal experience can help us to understand and contextualize our responses, often making overwhelming experience seem more manageable. Being able to communicate about our internal experience allows us to take care of ourselves by seeking help in managing our responses and by clearly expressing our wants and needs to other people.

We also want to help our clients to develop their sense of agency and control around management of these responses. Uncomfortable sensations and emotions often become more tolerable if we perceive that we have some choice over our experience. When we are integrating yoga-based practices into therapy, it is possible to provide clients with an opportunity to experience internal states without judgment, while at the same time providing an experience where they can learn that if things become painful, they can change what they are doing in ways that decrease the distress.

Our goal is to provide trauma survivors with a safe opportunity to challenge themselves through gentle yoga, and in doing so to transform their relationship to their bodies. We are working to create a balance between an acceptance of internal sensations and emotions that can provide us with useful information, and a sense of empowerment to create change in our lives. The more we can help people learn to listen to their bodies and recognize when a yoga exercise is causing pain, triggering a flashback, or activating a dissociative coping response, and the more we can empower them to make adjustments that relieve physical discomfort or restore a sense of safety, choice, and self-control, the more effectively they will be able to use yoga as a mechanism of healing in their overall process of trauma recovery.

BUILDING CURIOSITY: AN EXERCISE

If you like, gently drop your left ear toward your left shoulder. Allow this shift, this gesture, to be purposely gentle and slow, slow enough that you can have a chance to notice any sensation that arises. You may notice sensation in the right side of your neck, for example. This sensation is caused by muscles stretching. If you notice that it becomes uncomfortable at all, you can always decrease the sensation by lifting your head back toward neutral. You may even want to practice lifting your head slightly just as an experiment. What do you notice? Can you feel the sensation change according to the angle of your head? Feel free to pause for a few breaths on this side just to investigate sensation. When you are ready, gently shift back to neutral (head to center), and if you like, try the other side.

Changing the Relationship with the Body

> I have awareness in the days after class that I actually have a body.
> YOGA STUDENT at the Trauma Center

Trauma-sensitive yoga can help people befriend their bodies. Yoga involves creating a more tolerant, gentle approach to connecting with the body. It teaches people to move away from shutting down the body's reactions, or pushing the body to go beyond what it is able to tolerate; instead, it teaches people to connect with their bodies within an optimal "window of tolerance."[3] The window of tolerance refers to an individualized and fluid range of manageable affective, somatic, and cognitive arousal. Hyperarousal is an intense emotional experience that is outside of the window of tolerance, while numbing and dissociation are the shutting down or lack of emotional experiences that are outside of the window of tolerance. Each person has his or her own unique window of tolerance. Importantly, this window can narrow or enlarge over time, across contexts, or in response to changing life circumstances and events, including exposure to adversity or enhancement of individual capacities and resources.

Trauma survivors often have developed a highly constricted window of tolerance, in which even moderate emotions or physiological reactivity become untenable and serve to activate traumatic memories or trigger traumatogenic response states. Many trauma survivors have come to establish a harsh relationship with their bodies that involves self-harming through behaviors like drug and alcohol abuse, dysfunctional eating, and self-mutilation. Being in a body that has become attributed to be the source of so much pain and suffering is very difficult for many trauma survivors; sometimes, the only thing that makes sense is to punish this "failed" body over and over—in essence, repeating the trauma in one's subjective and objective relationship to one's body.

With trauma-sensitive yoga we are interested in helping people discover a different kind of relationship to their body—one that is gentler and more forgiving. A priority is placed on safety and health, and challenges to the body are approached with temperance. We are aware of just how challenging this task is; it requires us to practice patience and kindness over the long term.

Trauma-sensitive yoga practice also provides a way for us to investigate our habitual body patterns and explore new ways of being physical that we have not previously considered. Prolonged exposure to trauma can lock us into a few specific body patterns that may feel protective but become stifling and limiting over time. For some traumatize individuals, yoga offers a safe way to experiment with these patterns and discover healthier and more expansive ways of being embodied that in turn advance self-understanding, engender personal agency, and awaken possibility.

SEATED TWIST: BEFRIENDING YOUR BODY

If you like, let's begin in the Seated Mountain posture (see chapter 5). Notice your feet on the ground. Notice your tall spine. Notice some broadening and expansiveness across your chest. When you are ready, begin to turn gently to your left. If you like, you can bring your left hand to your left hip and your right hand across your left thigh. Turning very gently toward your left, see if you can maintain your feet on the ground, a tall spine, and a broadening and expansiveness across your chest. Feel free to give yourself a moment to breathe here. Notice that you do not have to turn very far. Maybe a slight turn works best. Make sure you can breathe comfortably and that there is no pain. If you feel any pain—any tension or discomfort whatsoever—please be willing to back down. You could experiment with coming out of the twist totally (you always have that control) or just backing down to the point where you can breathe comfortably. Feel free to experiment but, perhaps, making a commitment to feeling comfortable in the form. After a few breaths with the twist to your left, feel free to unwind through the middle and experiment with the other side in the same way. Adding something: *When you are turning to one side, you can experiment with turning your chin toward that shoulder and even glancing toward the wall behind you—drawing the twist through your eyes.* When you are ready, gently return back to the middle and to your Seated Mountain posture. Slowly open your eyes if they are closed.

Centering

For our purposes, a "center" is anything around which we organize ourselves physically, somatically, psychologically, and/or emotionally. In this context, a center can be our family, our job, our religious views, our community, or our health, as well as our ideas about the world, our psychological profile, and more. This center can also be internal, at the core of our bodies. Each human being, like all things, has a physical center that we can organize ourselves around. Our physical center establishes a point of reference for proprioception, the sense of where the parts of our body are in relation to each other. This physical center also helps us to maintain a sense of balance. In many Eastern perspectives, this organization around a center goes beyond the physical and implies a person who is stable, knows who they are, is balanced—we can imagine many more characteristics of the "centered person." It may be observed that many trauma survivors have lost this sense of an independent, stable center.

Consider the chronically abused children who must always attend to often unpredictable, often treacherous outside forces to gauge their safety and standing in the world. The abuser usurps the victim's right to have his or her own internal center from which to view the world. The abuser becomes the "center," and this may establish a pattern whereby survivors do not know how to look within for that sense of stability and safety. Trauma-sensitive yoga attempts to help people reconnect with this fundamental, internal, physical center.

For many trauma survivors, the trauma becomes the most powerful center around which they organize themselves. Because the experience of trauma may be the most important experience of our lives—changing us physically, physiologically, emotionally, and even spiritually—it can become an epicenter with intense gravitational pull. Much of the pain of trauma comes in its aftermath, through the repeated response to, reorganization around, and anticipation of the event(s). These post-traumatic sequelae can take the form of symptoms and survival strategies—like hypervigilance, hyperarousal, depression, numbing, and flashbacks—that are exhausting to one's body and spirit.

An essential element of trauma-sensitive yoga is to help people find other centers. We focus first and foremost on the physical center of the body—the core. The work is to help people find their physical center and to discover this powerful source of stability and strength right in their own body. This physical centering can expand to a sense of emotional balance and balance in one's life. We envision the yoga practice as something for trauma survivors to organize themselves around that is not only free of pain and suffering, but that is also a potential source of strength, well-being, and peacefulness. It is this sensibility that guides our centering practices in trauma-sensitive yoga.

FINDING YOUR CENTER

As you are ready, begin to notice how you are sitting in your chair. Start to get a feeling for your form. In particular, let's experiment with finding our center. One way to do this is to begin with some movements. You may choose to gently rock forward and back or side to side. You can also make these movements more circular. If you like, make these movements as big as they are going to be at first, and then gradually make them smaller and smaller. As you begin to make your movements smaller and smaller, you may also wish to experiment with making them slower and more deliberate. As you make your movements smaller and slower, you may notice muscles of your lower abdomen beginning to engage. Lower belly muscles may naturally start to brighten and activate. Take a moment to notice the quality of that muscular energy right at your center. Finally, if you like, you can interact with those core muscles by gently hugging or drawing in your lower belly to cultivate strength and stability right at your center. Pause for a moment if you like in order to investigate your center as a source of support and stability.

Another great way of learning about your center is to experiment with a balancing practice. One important note, however, is that with trauma-sensitive yoga we have moved away from the term *balance* in general and toward the term *centering*. To balance implies failure (either you stay up or you wobble and fall down), but with centering there is less space for failure because it is more of an internal investigation. In fact, if we are engaging in a centering practice, losing balance actually becomes a resource. This is because every time we stumble, our abdominal muscles naturally brighten and engage in order to help us back toward uprightness. We can learn so much about our center by stumbling. Consider the following presentation of a traditional balance exercise (The Tree) modified in order to emphasize the centering practice that is available.

THE TREE: A CENTERING PRACTICE

As you are ready, let's begin by standing up. You can have your shoes on or off—that is up to you. If you like, once you are standing, bring your palms together in front of your heart. Allow your breath to be free and easy. You may be breathing in and out through your nose or your mouth; for now it doesn't matter. When you are ready, begin to shift over to your left leg—start to bring your weight into your left foot and leg. You can keep your right toes on the ground if you like, or gently turn your right knee out and tuck your right foot up against your left ankle. Another option is to slide your right foot up to your left calf so you are entirely on one foot. You have many options. Feel free to take a moment to explore them. You may try something, and if that does not work, try something else. You are never stuck. You can always change your form. Now, take a moment to consider your gaze. You may choose to look at a point on the floor or the wall in front of you. For some of us it helps to pick a single point to look at, and to gently focus our gaze on that one point. Again, allow your breath to be free and easy. You may also experiment with looking at your fingertips (if your palms are together in front of your heart). Another "gaze" is to close your eyes and turn your attention inward. Closing your eyes may help you to begin to relate to your center. One way that we balance is to take in visual information from the world around us and to orient ourselves to that information. If you close your eyes, you will find other resources, most especially your center. Closing your eyes, even for a breath or two, can be a great way to start to relate to your center. Again, the suggestion is to gently hug in your lower belly if it is helpful. This centering practice is physical, visceral: right in your body right in this moment. If you like, take a moment to explore some muscular energy—strength and stability at your core. Finally, notice how this centering practice affects your balance. Is there any discernable effect when you orient yourself to your center? When you hug or gently draw in your lower belly?

Grounding

Dissociation is a response to overwhelming experience that can become habitual. In stressful situations, many trauma survivors simply "blank out" or "space out." While protective, this response mechanism can itself begin to create distress, particularly when it occurs outside of conscious control. Trauma-sensitive yoga can support the development of grounding strategies that can be used to combat dissociation. For instance, Mountain posture is considered to be a very "grounding" posture because of its focus on the connection to the earth, or the use of gravity as a sensory stimulus.

STANDING MOUNTAIN: A GROUNDING PRACTICE

Please note that while we are presenting this posture as a standing form, it could also be done seated or prone. The key is to help folks investigate where they are physically connected to the ground.

If you like, let's begin by standing up. You may have your shoes on or off—that is up to you. When you are ready, bring your feet flat onto the floor. Begin to notice your feet making contact with the floor. For a moment just focus on those spaces on your feet that you feel making contact with the floor. It may be one spot on one foot. It may be a more general, even unlocatable sensation for now. You may not have any sensation just now, and that is also okay. Just give yourself a little space for this noticing. Next, allowing your breath to be free and easy, shift your attention to your center. Hugging or gently drawing in your lower belly if it is helpful, begin to establish your center. (The facilitator may refer to the centering practice above for some cues.) Now with your feet on the ground and your center engaged, notice the very top of your head, the crown of your head. If you like, you can gently lift or articulate straight up through the crown of your head so that you are standing naturally tall. Finally, with your feet on the ground, your center engaged, and your spine naturally tall and upright, allow everything else to release. Let your shoulders drop gently. Allow the muscles in your face, your jaw, to let go. For a moment, get a sense of gravity at work in your body. Notice where you are grounded, supported by the earth. Notice where you are stable in your own body and where you can let go. Pause here for a few breaths if you like.

Building Affect-Regulation Skills

Trauma survivors frequently struggle with affect dysregulation, in which their emotions vacillate from one extreme to another. As we discussed in the earlier section on the physiological basis of the survival response, emotional states are tied to arousal level in the body. When we are dysregulated, our bodies often vacillate between hyperarousal and hypoarousal.

Trauma-sensitive yoga can help to build skills for both upregulation (increasing activation of the body) as well as down-regulation (calming the body). For example, if clients are slumped in their chairs, with very low energy, you can use yoga practices to try an energetic "experiment," exploring whether there is a shift in mood or feeling with an energizing practice. It could be as simple as moving from sitting to standing. Or, even in the chair, you could try experimenting with the Mountain postures described above. In another section, we will describe some breathing practices that may also be helpful. On the other hand, if your client is hyperaroused and has trouble sitting in the chair or is breathing rapidly, you may want to experiment together with some calming practices. Here's one that may be helpful:

SEATED FORWARD FOLD: A CALMING PRACTICE

If you like, bring your feet a little farther apart than your hips. As you begin to experiment with this forward fold, you have many options. You can lean your forearms into your thighs—this may be enough of a forward fold. You can also bring your fingertips to the floor, or maybe your hands to the floor. Another option is to take one hand to the opposite elbow and hang freely forward. Feel free to experiment with these options for a moment. You can try something, and if that does not work, try something else. Take a moment to experiment. If you like, when you are ready, you may wish to gently shake your head yes and no, allowing the muscles in your neck and upper back to release a little bit. You may also choose to gently move your jaw in a way that invites any tension in your jaw to release. Feel free to breathe here for about twenty seconds. When you are ready, begin to move gently back toward your upright Seated Mountain posture, allowing your breath to be free and easy.

Please keep in mind that what is calming for one person may be very upsetting for someone else. Ask for feedback, and use your own best judgment to determine the efficacy of this or any exercise in the book. Remember, subjective experiences are more important than anything else when it comes to the trauma-sensitive yoga practice.

Breathing Practices and Affect Regulation

Breathing exercises can be a powerful tool for affect regulation—that is, changing the way you feel right in your body, in the moment. When the survival response is activated, breathing often becomes more rapid and shallow, increasing oxygen throughout the body. Survivors of chronic trauma often develop shallow breathing patterns, consistent with anxiety, hyperarousal, or panic states. When they are triggered or overwhelmed, many trauma survivors also tend to hold their breath, often unconsciously. Holding the breath is defensive and can be a protection against overwhelming emotion. However, these breathing patterns leave our bodies in a state of tension and dysregulation and may add to the overall sense of unease in the body that many trauma survivors experience. Breathing can be a way of making contact with the self. It can be used for up-regulation (energizing) or down-regulation (calming). Finding and experimenting with new ways of breathing may be a way for folks to feel better in their bodies.

From the yoga perspective, breathing practice (pranayam) is fairly advanced and comes with many cautions. In general, we are very careful with breathing techniques and recommend that students attempt most breathing practices under the guidance of a qualified teacher. Some survivors may feel triggered by breathing more deeply and letting down the body's defenses. Other people may feel triggered by more rapid breathing techniques that are used in some forms of yoga. The breathing practices we present in this book may be comfortable for readers to try at home, in a therapy office, or in a class, but we always recommend that our clients listen to their bodies and stop if they feel uncomfortable for any reason.

In general, our approach to breathing in the context of traumasensitive yoga is to help people gently expand their capacity for breath—to find a little more space for breath in their body. We have found that for many of our students, working with breath is very challenging and is best approached cautiously and with a great deal of patience. A tiny shift can feel like a huge leap, and we would rather have folks slowly acclimate to breathing a little deeper as they feel comfortable than jump in too quickly and become uncomfortable.

One practice we often invite students to experiment with we call "Adding a Little Breath." The instruction is something like "if you like, you may wish to experiment with adding a little to your in-breath and a little to your out-breath. You may be breathing through your nose or through your mouth, it doesn't matter for this practice. Simply beginning with your breath as it is, if you like, experiment with adding a little to your inhale and a little to your exhale." This practice has been a way for many students to begin to experiment with gently expanding their capacity for breath in an accessible and safe way.

Note: It can be a very powerful experience for trauma survivors to find new tools to regulate their physiological or affective experiences. The exercises we present here are meant as illustrative examples only; if these exercises do not create the outcome you are working toward, continue to use creativity and experimentation with your clients and see if you can find some that do.

Practicing Choice

I like the repetition of choice.

I appreciate that there is no right or wrong and that there are no expectations.

The choice is empowering.

YOGA STUDENTS at the Trauma Center

We devote space in this book to a theme we call "Practice Making Choices." However, we feel this is such an important theme in the context of trauma-sensitive yoga that we wanted to say a few words to clinicians about choice. For survivors, it may feel like there are no options, especially when it comes to being in pain—"pain" in a very global sense—and that there is nothing one can do about this state of pain and unease. The yoga postures can provide small, manageable experiences where we can begin to question these assumptions, where we can begin to investigate making choices in relation to pain. We are able to practice gaining feedback from our body, and then have a successful experience of noticing that the choices we make lead to freeing up that pain in the moment. We're keeping it very clearly focused on the experience and the posture at hand, but the overall effect may be that we gently challenge those deep assumptions that there is never ever anything we can do to relieve pain.

We want to encourage you to give your clients many opportunities to make choices for themselves. No matter what exercise you are doing, we suggest that you specifically invite your clients to make choices with regard to the experience they are having in their body. If you agree with Judith Herman's idea that creating a sense of power and agency is central to the recovery of trauma survivors, you might wish to experiment with yoga-based interventions that can give your clients a unique opportunity to practice choice as a concrete experience with consequences right in the moment, rather than exploring choice as an abstract idea. If I choose to make my shoulder circles a little smaller, I may notice right then that I experience no pain in the action. If I choose to lift my leg a tiny bit higher in the seated leg lift, I may feel some core muscles in my belly engage right then. For the folks we work with, there is often a tremendous rift between what is happening in their body and the choices they are making. They experience a disconnection from their bodies because they feel they are stuck in various states of discomfort without any options. They often develop a chronic lack of interest in what ultimately happens to their body: "There is nothing I can do to make myself feel better, so why bother?" With yoga, we give trauma survivors a chance to experience making choices that may or may not have a positive outcome in their body in the moment. One client at the Trauma Center told us, "You can't say the word 'choice' enough." This leads us to suggest that you repeatedly use the word "choice" with your clients when experimenting with yoga-based interventions.

EMPOWERMENT THROUGH MAKING CHOICES

Here is a choice practice that you are welcome to try at any point during these exercises. Notice if what you are doing is painful in any way or if you sense that you are hurting yourself, and then make the choice to stop. Change what you are doing so that you are no longer hurting yourself. For example, if you are doing a neck roll and you notice that your neck hurts, make the choice to stop hurting yourself by making the movement smaller or stopping altogether. For this practice, you are aware that you are choosing to stop hurting yourself. This is a very powerful practice, and it is always available to you. Your body will remember the commitment you have made to protect yourself from pain in this moment.

Integrating Aspects of Experience

In order to avoid pain, it can be adaptive to disconnect from some aspects of experience. However, because of this disconnection, trauma survivors may experience their world, and aspects of themselves, as disjointed and lacking a sense of coherence. We introduced this concept earlier when we discussed creating rhythms, a key component of trauma-sensitive yoga. Trauma-sensitive yoga can allow you to practice integrating different aspects of your experience. For instance, yoga coordinates movement from posture to posture with intake and outflow of the breath.[4] Movement and breath are also coordinated among people who are practicing yoga together. In this practice, we are integrating our kinesthetic sense (sense of movement) with exteroceptive senses (external senses), such as hearing our breaths in our ears, and with interoceptive senses (senses that are stimulated from within the body), such as noticing our heart rates increasing. The focus on this integration creates a sense of "flow," in which different aspects of experience becomes interrelated.[5] Here is a flow-oriented exercise that emphasizes the integration of breath and movement:

SUN BREATHS: INTEGRATING BREATH AND MOVEMENT

Note: This exercise involves developing intrapersonal rhythms, discussed in chapter 4.

From your Seated or Standing Mountain posture, let's begin to practice integrating breath and movement. As you inhale, begin to sweep your arms up, and with your exhale draw your palms through the center. On your inhale, make a circle with your arms, and on your exhale draw your palms together through the middle of that circle. This can be a grand, sweeping gesture. For some folks, this may be too much. You can practice integrating breath and movement with a small gesture, such as beginning with your hands on your thighs. On your inhale, lift your hands an inch or two, and on your exhale return you hands to your thighs. For a moment, let's try coordinating our breath and movement together so that we are both moving and breathing to the same rhythm. (Both parties may want to take turns setting the pace.) Finally, take a moment to find your own rhythm, breathing and moving at your own pace. When you are ready, let's come back to a comfortable, seated posture.

Increasing Confidence

Being hurt repeatedly can lead to a sense of helplessness and powerlessness. Some survivors have used a submission-based survival response for many years, ignoring their own wants or needs in order to placate the demands of others. They may become confused about how they actually feel, or what they want. In addition, because many trauma survivors struggle with self-blame, they have learned not to trust themselves and their own instincts.

Because of this loss of self-trust, a primary goal for survivors might be to rebuild their sense of confidence and empowerment. Regular yoga practice increases strength and flexibility, both physically and mentally. These shifts can lead practitioners toward an increased sense of confidence in their ability to address challenges.

As a specific illustration, let's consider the dynamic of moving from sitting to standing. Especially in a therapy office, where most of the interaction takes place sitting in chairs, it can be profoundly empowering to practice postural shifts as a way of increasing confidence. This can be especially helpful if the therapist and/or client have identified feelings of powerlessness or dissociative responses as a struggle for the client. This somatic strategy may be integrated into ongoing clinical work that focuses on the issue of empowerment, or it may be a completely new somatic experience that raises new clinical issues ("I didn't realize how collapsed and disconnected I felt sitting in the chair until I stood up tall"). In either case, introducing a somatic practice aimed at exploring, challenging, and shifting feelings of powerlessness may be very helpful.

Please consider this reflection from a yoga student at the Trauma Center on her experience of building confidence through yoga:

> At my last yoga session, I internalized the idea that I can modify my postures and environment to suit my needs. Mentally I had heard it over and over, but physically I never felt I had the power to take action. Thank you for telling me that it was OK and a good thing when I made the necessary changes in my postures, and thank you for providing a more comfortable environment for my practice.... Gaining the confidence to move away from the pain in the yoga practice helped me to move away from the pain of my past. I'm feeling good now; I feel strong.

FINDING STRENGTH WITHIN

If you like, take a moment to notice that you are sitting. You may be aware of your posture in the chair at this moment. Just take note of whether you are sitting back in the chair, sitting forward, or leaning to one side. The object here is not to judge one posture as better than any other but simply to notice how you are physically sitting in your chair at this moment. If judgment comes up, that is OK. Again, maybe practice just noticing the judgment and, if you can, come back to the practice of noticing the pure physicality of sitting. After a moment, when you are ready, slowly begin to stand up. The invitation here is to move slowly and deliberately. Feel your feet begin to take your body weight. Notice, if your chair has arms, that you may use your hands and upper body to help you transition. Staying close to the physical experience for the moment, as you unfold from your chair, you may feel some muscles begin to engage that were not activated when you were sitting. What's happening in your legs? What's happening in your back? What's happening with your core abdominal muscles? Are there any other muscles that you notice? Once you are fully standing, perhaps pause for a moment and take a few breaths.

For the therapist, facilitator, or practitioner, you may want to use the script for Standing Mountain here, or you may want to continue as follows.

Simply give yourself a moment to stand and breathe. It can be as simple as that. A suggestion is to use a clock or to simply count slowly for thirty seconds (you can choose another period of time if you like) to stand and breathe. When that time period is up, feel free to return to a seated position in your chair.

Building Connection to Others

> The experience of doing the class with others is helpful; I feel like I am not alone.
> YOGA STUDENT at the Trauma Center

Judith Herman writes, "The core experiences of psychological trauma are disempowerment and disconnection from others. Recovery, therefore, is based upon the empowerment of the survivor and the creation of new connections."[6] Trauma-sensitive yoga can be a way to practice reconnection right in the office. Although it may be very helpful to connect with and support clients around their traumatic experiences, this is not the full extent of connection with another human being. It may be extremely helpful to be heard by your therapist, but this is different from having a shared experience. We suggest that another layer of reconnection occurs in the process of creating a shared experience, in doing something together such as trauma-sensitive yoga.

Yoga is a nonverbal tradition that is often undertaken in groups. Similar to group-oriented sports or dance, integrated movement with others can create a sense of connection that transcends language. These benefits may be realized even in the context of a one-on-one practice in the therapy office. Clients and therapists often fall into distinct roles that may not cultivate this sense of shared human experience. We suggest that, without compromising your therapeutic boundaries, you can bring some shared human experience into the office through these yoga practices. One way to practice such a visceral connection in the office is to purposefully move and breathe together, in rhythmical sync. In order for this to work, the "leader" of the exercise needs to check in with the other(s) involved to make sure that the pace she or he sets is comfortable, and then needs to be able to respond to feedback accordingly. In fact, this may be a good opportunity for each person to be the "leader" (the one setting the pace), to have the experience of being mirrored or followed, and for each person to be attended to as the "follower." Feel free to experiment with these roles in the Sun Breath variation practice below.

NONVERBAL CONNECTION THROUGH A SUN BREATH VARIATION

This exercise focuses on the nonverbal connection between people who are moving and breathing together. One person will start off as the leader, and the other person will be the follower. The leader will guide the practice and can set the pace for a number of cycles, say fifteen, or a set duration of time, say thirty seconds. You might want to determine these parameters together before beginning the exercise. This exercise is particularly well suited to alternating the "leader" and "follower" roles so that you can explore the differences in what it feels like to be the leader versus the follower.

Note: This exercise reiterates one of the key themes in trauma-sensitive yoga: building rhythms. See chapter 4 for more about interpersonal rhythms.

If you like, please come into your Seated Mountain posture. With your hands on your thighs or toward your knees, as you inhale, gently stretch your arms out to the sides. As you exhale, bring your palms together in front of your heart, and then bring your hands back to your thighs or knees. Inhale, stretch; exhale, bring together; and gently release.

As you breathe and move together, feel free to notice not only your own individual experience of connecting your breath and your movement, but also the experience of breathing and moving together. If you like, really focus on that shared experience. When you are ready, perhaps return to your Seated Mountain posture and sit quietly for a few breaths together with the eyes open or closed.

Addressing Challenges in Introducing Yoga-Based Strategies into the Therapy Office

Clinicians often come to us with concerns that their clients are reluctant to participate in body-based interventions because it is an uncomfortable or unpleasant experience for them, particularly initially. Clients may also be embarrassed by moving their bodies in session, and by being "seen." Clinicians also ask us how to avoid triggering their clients when using yoga-based interventions. One caveat up front is that we know that we cannot eliminate all triggers; in fact, we believe that it is not our job to do so. Ultimately, we hope to create a safe space for people to confront triggers and deal with them effectively when they arise. We recognize that survivors sometimes respond to challenging situations (such as experimenting with body-based interventions) through dissociation. Dissociation has been an effective coping skill for many of our clients for many years and will continue to serve a purpose. We also know that constant dissociation can be debilitating and dangerous. With yoga, perhaps we can offer some other tools (such as grounding skills or affect-regulation strategies) for addressing triggers that may end up being safer and more effective.

Renee's story illustrates how a clinician responded to a client's triggered response while she was experimenting with chair-based yoga practices in a therapy session. The challenge for Renee and her therapist was to turn what could have felt like a failure into a learning experience that could facilitate further growth.

RENEE'S STORY

Renee grew up in an abusive and chaotic household. Her father was an alcoholic who became a violent tyrant when he was drinking. He was often physically abusive to Renee's older brother Martin, and verbally and emotionally abusive to Renee and her mother. Martin directed his helpless rage toward Renee, particularly when their parents were not around. Renee described her mother as a "ghost" who did not seem to notice much of what was happening and who was completely unable to protect Renee. Renee recalled living in constant fear as a child. As an adult, Renee suffered from intense anxiety and had nightmares almost every night. She avoided relationships because she was not able to tolerate someone else seeing her or becoming close to her. She wondered if she were becoming a ghost like her mother.

Renee's therapist introduced yoga-based practices into the therapy. Some of their goals for therapy included increasing Renee's awareness of and ability to regulate her internal states. Renee was able to engage in Seated Mountain and to bring a sense of curiosity about her internal states. She noticed that her muscles were tight all throughout her body, particularly in her shoulders. She noticed a clenched sensation in her abdomen and a tightness in her chest.

Renee's therapist next moved to introducing a breathing practice along with the Seated Mountain posture. She participated in the exercises with Renee. They each put a hand over their chests and over their abdomens and worked on abdominal breathing ("belly breaths"). After several increasingly deep breaths, Renee became very anxious. She described feeling her heart beating rapidly and feeling overwhelmed, and she began to cry.

Renee's therapist worked with Renee to help ground her, by having her feel her feet on the floor, and feeling the gravity keeping her in contact with her chair. Renee slowly calmed down and became more present in the room.

Renee and her therapist debriefed the exercise and reviewed how each portion of the exercise had felt to Renee. Renee began to understand that feeling relaxed actually created a sense of anxiety for her. Renee's therapist was able to help normalize her experience and to provide a framework for

Renee to understand that her hypervigilance is her body's way of trying to make sure that she is safe and protected.

Instead of perceiving this exercise as a failure, Renee and her therapist were able to explore together what they had learned from experimenting with this practice. Renee's somatic experience in the room helped them to name an internal conflict over one of Renee's goals for therapy: affect regulation. Although a part of Renee wanted to experience a sense of calm and a release of tension and anxiety, another part of her felt the need to be constantly on the alert for potential danger. The exercise helped Renee and her therapist refine their pacing in therapy, as well as their choices for intervention. They continued to strengthen Renee's confidence with mindfulness-based practices. They worked on regulation exercises that did not involve a "letting go" of control, such as increasing and decreasing the intensity of a felt emotion. They also worked on empowerment-based yoga exercises (such as moving from Seated to Standing Mountain posture), and resource building. When they returned to breathing exercises several months later, Renee had developed a greater sense of control over her own body and emotions and was less triggered by letting go of some of that control.

seven

For Yoga Teachers

Building a Trauma-Sensitive Yoga Class[1]

In some ways it gave me an incredible sense of freedom to do each pose in my own way because I couldn't do them in the usual way. I felt more embodied than I ever have in a class.

YOGA STUDENT at the Trauma Center

I wanted to share some ways in which the course affected me the last week and a half. I found it very interesting to hear myself in my classes saying, "When you are ready..." and "In your own time...," etc, without even thinking twice. It made me wonder—was I even offering such freedom of choice before? The teaching felt very different for me, and I loved it. I also found myself talking about yoga in a different way this week. With some of the scientific support, I heard a different confidence in my voice when explaining yoga's many benefits to nonpractitioners. I recognize that not everyone wants to hear about the more philosophical side of yoga initially, so having another angle with which to discuss it was exciting.

EMILY, yoga teacher, on her training with the Trauma Center

In an earlier chapter, we shared Kate's story with you. What should have been healing for Kate ended up triggering a trauma reaction. The class that she attended was not adapted to meet her unique needs. We believe that yoga has something important to offer to Kate and to other people who have had similar experiences. Now imagine for a moment that Kate worked with her therapist for several months, and is ready for another attempt at a yoga class. You are the teacher, and Kate walks into the room. What type of an experience would you want to be able to offer her?

We realized we would need to significantly modify the typical yoga class in order to create safety. We have developed a framework, "Domains of a Yoga Class," that we use to help us modify our yoga classes to be able to call them trauma-sensitive. We have identified five domains of a yoga class that need to be modified in order for the class to be trauma-sensitive: language, assists, teacher qualities, environment, and exercises.

Language

The words you speak. Your tone of voice. Your inflection. These are all considerations under the language domain. Trauma survivors are often attentive not only to what is said, but also to how it is expressed. When we are developing our linguistic style in teaching a yoga class, we can reflect on the fact that we are cultivating within our students the ability to slow down and to experience each moment in time. Our language can reflect and support that priority. Using a slow, soothing tone of voice will help to foster a calm atmosphere of healing. We also want to assist students in moving away from self-judgment, and toward an attitude of curiosity and interest in their own internal experiences.

Trauma-sensitive language tends to be concrete and gently brings attention to visceral experiences. We are not asking trauma survivors to imagine some out-of-body state (such as might occur through the use of imagery), but rather to experience what's happening in their body right now. We use metaphors very sparingly and suggest that trauma-sensitive language should gently but clearly direct attention to internal experiences while also inviting mindful moving and breathing.

There are two basic styles of language that we use at the Trauma Center Yoga Program: *language of inquiry* and *invitatory language*. Language of inquiry includes key words and phrases like "notice," "be curious," "approach with interest," "allow," "experiment," "feel," and other similar words. The language of inquiry promotes a mindful approach to yoga, in which there is no right or wrong, just experimentation and curiosity. We suggest that the yoga teacher use these words as much as possible to promote this sort of mindful stance in your students.

The other important language category is invitatory language, which is used to promote choice and control, two very important issues for trauma survivors. We are working to build a sense of empowerment within our students over their own bodies and their own experiences. They are in control of making the ultimate decisions about what feels right to them. As long as there are no issues of safety involved, we want to step back and let our students assert this control.

Our suggestion is to minimize the use of commands and veer toward invitation as much as possible. That said, there will be several times throughout the yoga class where a simple clear instruction will be best—"bring your knee right over your ankle" in Warrior One, for example. Clear instructions are most important when issues of safety are relevant, such as the potential for knee injury with overextension in Warrior One. Still, our work is to support trauma survivors as they develop a safe and ultimately friendly relationship with their bodies, and we have found that invitatory language best suits this purpose. Invitatory language includes phrases like "as you are ready," "if you like," "when you feel ready," and so on. This language emphasizes that the students are in control of their experience and that they can interact with the postures we are offering at their own pace. They are also free to choose not to do something if they are not ready. Another tip regarding the use of language is that it's better to give one instruction three times than three instructions once. Students may well miss what you say the first time, and even the second. It's OK to be repetitive. Remember that dissociation may occur frequently in the yoga class—triggers come and are unavoidable. By repeating instructions, you are offering a touchstone for students. The sound of your voice, and the guidance that you are offering in prompts, can assist students in coming back to the present moment.

Assists

There are at least three types of assists that a yoga teacher can offer her students: visual assists (modeling), verbal assists, and physical assists. The types of assists that you use within a trauma-sensitive yoga class should be carefully considered.

Visual assists occur when the instructor models a certain posture for students. We have gotten feedback from students that they often feel intimidated by how flexible the instructors are. This indicates that the instructors are modeling quite challenging postures. We would suggest that, in a trauma-sensitive yoga class, the modeling be directed toward lower intensity postures, and toward adaptations that the instructor is choosing to use to make the experience more feasible for all students. This type of assistance emphasizes that what is "right" or "best" is for each student to identify what is right or best for themselves as individuals, and not to "succeed" in doing the most challenging posture (and then experiencing injury or intense soreness later).

Verbal assists are also a constant part of a trauma-sensitive yoga class. Verbal assists can be very valuable and will show that you are attending to your students in an appropriate and nurturing way, while respecting their physical space and the integrity of those boundaries (i.e., you might suggest to try a block or blanket to make a posture more accessible). Verbal assists can be used for safety-based modifications, and they can also be used for encouragement. They can range from general reminders to students that "you have control over what you are doing with your body," to very specific guidance such as, "try bringing your knee just over your ankle in order to protect the joint." The trauma-sensitive yoga teacher can use words to show the students that they are being attended to and that the person in authority genuinely cares about their health and well-being. This can be a corrective experience for students who have never experienced being noticed and cared for by someone who has respect for their boundaries and personal space. It can also help to cultivate a safe, stable, predictable, and healthy relationship between the teacher and each student.

While visual and verbal assists can be freely used, in the context of trauma-sensitive yoga, physical assists are considered a clinical issue. For the yoga teacher to put her or his hands on a student is a serious decision that bears thoughtful deliberation. Consider the fact that many forms of trauma involve some sort of physical violation. Psychological abuse often includes intrusiveness on the part of the perpetrator and a lack of safe boundaries. Even chronic childhood neglect, like that experienced by so many of our students at the Trauma Center, often involves a crucial withholding of safe, healthy touch from caregivers. If we ever decide to offer physical assists, we must be very clear about what we are doing and why in order for it to be a healthy, empowering experience for our students.

Whether or not to offer physical assists has been an ongoing topic of discussion among the yoga teachers and the clinicians at the Trauma Center. We have been tempted to rule it out all together, but in some instances a student has found it incredibly helpful to receive the safe, stabilizing, physical support of the yoga teacher.

Our main concerns around physical assists are (1) that the student will interpret the touch as a traumatic reminder and may experience overwhelming emotions, intrusive memories, or dissociative flashbacks and (2) that the yoga teacher will actually use touch as a way to influence a student's experience because it is more expedient than inviting the student to have her or his own experience. As we began talking about this issue in detail, we realized that many of us had experienced touch as helpful and supportive in a yoga class. But we also realized that at least as many of us had experienced touch as something negative: unsolicited, aggressive, and uncontrollable, and for the teacher's benefit rather than our own.

Let's consider this last observation for a moment. Many of us have experienced touch from a yoga teacher at one time or another as coming from the teacher's need for the class to go a certain way and for the postures to be "performed" in the way that the teacher saw fit. In a trauma-sensitive context, this is really dangerous. While safety is always a priority for our program, we also want to help trauma survivors reclaim their bodies and their experiences as their own. Anything that takes away from the student's empowerment within the class is at best unhelpful, and at worst destructive.

Having investigated these very serious cautions for ourselves, we still decided to keep the possibility of physical assists available in our trauma-sensitive classes. We made the decision that we do not want to deny our students the possibility of positive human contact, as long as it is invited and done in a safe way. What follows are some considerations for the trauma-sensitive yoga teacher regarding physical assists.

At the Trauma Center, we make the following statements to our yoga students. We concentrate primarily on visual and verbal assists in this class. We will always ask before offering any sort of physical assist, and we only do so after students have had a chance to become comfortable in the class and with the instructor. We maintain an environment in which *the student can always say*

As an instructor, be very clear that the student has control over any physical interaction, and never do physical assists unless you have known the student for a while—we suggest at least several months. You may wish to have a conversation with students to determine who is comfortable with physical assists, or you may want to include a similar question on an intake form. Comment boxes are also helpful for soliciting this type of feedback from students.

There are several types of physical assists in a yoga class, but we will focus on three, which we will identify as follows: safety assists, comfort assists, and deepening assists. We would recommend using physical assists primarily for safety purposes in a trauma-sensitive yoga class;

for example, you may choose to use a physical assist if a student's knee is way "out of whack" (extended well beyond the ankle) in Warrior pose. You may even try a verbal assist a few times first and then offer the physical assist as a last resort. Be aware of your emotional state and what you are conveying to the student as you offer assists. Patience and kindness are always helpful. Remember that there are many reasons why students may not be able to translate the verbal cue into a physical action in their bodies. Make sure that you check in with yourself and remind yourself that what you are doing is *offering* a physical assist and that the student has total control in terms of whether or not to accept your offer. Approach the student from the front to avoid startling him or her, make eye contact, and be totally willing to accept his or her decision regarding your offer. Be as clear as possible with the student about exactly what you are offering. For instance, you may ask, "May I put my right hand on your knee and gently press, so that you can get a sense of what it feels like when your knee is directly over your ankle?"

Comfort assists, such as a gentle head cradle in Savasana, are assists that have no safety concerns attached at all and are totally oriented toward putting a student more at ease in a pose. Similarly, deepening assists, such as a hand on the lower back to create a deeper stretch in Downward-Facing Dog, are not oriented toward safety issues. The focus for deepening assists is, rather, to encourage the practitioner to intensify the posture. Comfort assists and deepening assists pose huge challenges in a trauma-sensitive context because we really do not know what will make each individual more or less comfortable, or when a stretch will feel too intense. For some of our students, a gentle touch on the shoulder can be a huge trigger and may lead to a dissociative flashback.

In one yoga class the teacher, who happened to be a substitute, decided to offer a student a comfort assist. The teacher, a female, came up behind a student while most of the class was lying down in a traditional Savasana form and gently cradled the student's head. The lights were low, the teacher's voice was soft, and this was the end of a yoga class—time to rest. The teacher explained to the student what the assist was and asked if it was OK. The student replied that, yes, it was. It turned out that the student was OK with the assist and actually found it helpful. The problem was with the student on the next mat over. She was a survivor of chronic childhood abuse, including sexual abuse in which her mother was the perpetrator. To see a woman come up behind her fellow student in the dim light and put her hands on her neck was enough to shake this student's confidence in the teacher and to raise serious doubts for her about the safety of the class. This particular teacher was a substitute, and the regular teacher did not offer such assists, so it was unexpected for the student to witness this type of interaction. It truly makes you wonder about the meaning of a "comfort" assist. After the class, the student who was triggered was able to talk to her therapist and to the regular yoga teacher, so we were able to respond appropriately as a team and work to help this student reestablish a feeling of safety in the space.

A key principle here regarding any type of assist is that we do not want to impose our will on our students. We are attempting to help students develop self-knowledge and a more positive relationship with their own bodies. It may be that, after a time, physical assists can serve these ends, but that is not necessarily or always true. Remember the words of Dr. Judith Herman: "No intervention that takes power away from the survivor can possibly foster her recovery, no matter how much it appears to be in her immediate best interest." Any time we are assisting students, we should be assisting them in developing a sense of empowerment and control over themselves.

Teacher Qualities

This domain refers to how yoga teachers handle themselves in the room, from the clothing we choose to the way we manage our bodies in the physical space. We will also include some discussion about class management and class dynamics. Before we get into this section, we want to take a moment to reiterate the message that we offered to therapists about self-awareness and self-care. As a person who is supporting the healing of others, your somatic and emotional states are of utmost importance. Many trauma survivors are highly attuned to the nuances of the emotional states of others. Please take the time to make sure that you are in a calm and self-aware state before each class.

We have found that a successful trauma-sensitive yoga teacher is one who is present and light (smiles from time to time), as opposed to being heavy and negative; who is engaged, welcoming, and approachable; and who is very competent and at ease with the yoga material but invites feedback and is willing to listen—*and to make appropriate changes in relation to that feedback.* These qualities reflect your wellness and are inviting for your students.

Yoga teachers in a trauma-sensitive context might want to dress conservatively to minimize any distractions and to minimize triggers. For example, a male teacher in an all-female class was asked by students not to wear spandex shorts. Be aware that the issue of appropriate clothing may come up for class members as well. You may want to consider offering some guidance about apparel prior to the first class.

We suggest that the teacher be in the room before students arrive and have the space set up adequately to avoid any rushing around (see the next section for more details about the environment domain). Consider extending a verbal "welcome" to each student for each class either individually or to the group as a whole. Students have made a great effort to come to the space, and we have found that they may not know they are welcome unless they are told. We can convey to them that they are simply welcome, with no other expectations.

A trauma-sensitive yoga teacher does not move around during the class very much, and students know where to locate her or him at any point throughout the class (no surprises!). If you do need to move to adjust the temperature or to let someone in, the suggestion is that you tell students exactly what you are doing and why: "I am going to adjust the temperature because a few people have mentioned that it is too hot."

In terms of how yoga teachers manage the class, we suggest that you do not call students out by name. We have found that even if teachers call students out for praise, the experience of having your name said aloud in a trauma-sensitive yoga class can be shaming. If a teacher feels like it is important to acknowledge something positive about a student's practice, that feedback can be given one to one at the end of class.

Praise can also be problematic in a trauma-sensitive yoga class because it may communicate to students that pleasing the teacher is more important than paying attention to their own subjective experience. We do not want to give this message. We want to deeply honor the subjective experience of the student above everything else. Sometimes this can mean allowing folks to have a difficult experience and not trying to call it anything else. We have had the experience of calling someone's posture "great" when their personal experience was that they were not comfortable in the form. This sort of disconnect can be very confusing and may inadvertently discourage students from simply attending to and honoring their internal or somatic experience. There may be space for praise, but we do suggest caution. We encourage you to think carefully about why you have the urge to praise someone and to deeply consider whether or not your words will be helpful.

Another situation where we have seen problems arise is when the yoga teacher approaches the class with the attitude of a "trauma expert." For instance, a teacher might say something like, "This form is difficult for trauma survivors" or "This posture should feel really good." Our work is to present opportunities for experience, but not to dictate what the subjective experience should be. Our work as trauma-sensitive yoga teachers is to cultivate a safe, stable, predictable environment in which our students can have their own experience and then to do our best to support that. In teaching trauma-sensitive yoga, the job of the yoga teacher is not to create artificial challenges—many of our students have already challenged themselves more than we may ever know just by showing up. The work of the teacher is to cultivate enough safety so that students can challenge themselves as they are ready, and in ways that feel safe.

Environment

This domain refers to the physical space in which the yoga class occurs and includes cleanliness, lighting, privacy, temperature, and music options among other things. One yoga teacher was teaching a yoga class on a military base, and the space for the class was located very close to a rifle range. For marines who had just returned from Iraq and Afghanistan, this was not ideal. Still, she was able to create a safe, predictable space for her students.

A yoga class at a residential school for adolescents was set up in the recreation room, which was located right next to some "timeout" rooms where kids could take themselves if they were really upset—and they would get upset during yoga class once in a while! Not ideal, but still the space became safe enough for students to rest comfortably in Savasana.

If you decide to teach trauma-sensitive yoga, you may be going into institutional settings or other settings that were not developed to be safe, calm, quiet, and predictable. In reality, you will do your best to attend to the environment and make do with what is available. Don't be afraid to show up early, grab a broom and a mop (like one teacher who led a class in a lunch room), and clean up. This effort is better than practicing yoga with gum on the floor and shows your students that you care enough to give them a clean space in which to practice yoga.

In terms of lighting, some rooms have one light switch, so it's all or nothing. We suggest that if you have a choice between bright lights and very low lights, you go with the bright lights. Dark or dim rooms tend to be more triggering than bright rooms. Ideally, you would want to find something in between, where the lights are on, but it is not glaring. You may consider bringing in lamps or other soft lighting if your only other option is harsh overhead fluorescents. We suggest that you do not change the lighting during the course of the class. Some yoga teachers will turn lights off during Savasana, for example. We have found this to be very disturbing for many of our students. If students decide to close their eyes during Savasana, and the lights are turned off, students may be triggered by the unexpected darkness when they open their eyes again. Again, the circumstances surrounding the trauma differ from individual to individual, but we have found that for many of our students, a dim or dark room tends to be troubling for more folks than is a brightly lit room and that changing the lighting, especially from light to dark, tends to be more disturbing than simply leaving lights on during Savasana.

Ideally, we would not want a trauma-sensitive class to have open, exposed windows. In one setting, the teacher needed to find a foldable, portable screen to place in front of some public windows before each class. Do your best to limit people walking in and out of the room inadvertently during the class (e.g., maintenance or delivery). Try to minimize external noise, but if noises occur, try to name them: "That was a large truck that just went by," or "Sounds like there is some construction going on outside today." The idea is to help your students stay grounded in the present moment. Some important symptoms of PTSD to understand in this regard are hypervigilance (being constantly on the alert for danger), an exaggerated startle response (being jumpy or easily startled), triggered responses (being reminded of the trauma), or flashbacks (feeling like the traumatic event is happening again). Dissociative flashback episodes can be triggered by noises similar to those present during a traumatic event. During one yoga class for veterans, there was a jackhammer going just outside the yoga space. In this case, the teacher witnessed the somatic (body-based) distress of her students and asked the construction workers to stop. In another instance with the same class, a vehicle with a siren went by. Sirens are prevalent in some war zones and are potentially triggering. This time, the teacher just named the event ("Sounds like a fire truck just drove by the studio") and returned to the yoga practice. She noted that her students seemed to relax after that comment, and she decided that her brief intervention was enough in that particular situation. See the section "Responding to Triggered Reactions in a Yoga Class" later in this chapter for more on yoga-based strategies for triggers such as dissociative flashbacks.

Our general approach in terms of the environment involves seeking out feedback from our students and not making any changes to the environment without consulting them. Maybe more than in your regular yoga studio class, consider your students in your traumasensitive yoga classes as collaborators, and give them as much control over the environment as possible.

Exercises

All of the exercises we practice are focused on the goal of helping trauma survivors reclaim and develop a friendliness with their bodies—not on achieving a perfection of alignment or form (though those things may come, and we wouldn't want to rule them out!). With this in mind, the exercises domain still focuses on the postures themselves and includes posture choice, posture progression, and the timing and pacing of your class (how many cues you give for a particular form versus how much silence).

Let's tackle the most obvious first: we would not want to introduce a challenging posture, such as the prone hip-opening Happy Baby, in the first class. We recognize that postures pose not only physical challenges, but psychological challenges as well. There may be great value in a posture such as Happy Baby, but we would want to work up to it over the course of several months, beginning with a seated hip opener, for example. The first hip opener may be Janu Sirsasana (head-to-knee forward bend). You could also introduce the idea of hip openers in something strong like a lunge or a Warrior pose.

As trauma-sensitive yoga teachers, we would hope for every single yoga posture to be accessible to our students eventually. However, we recognize that certain postures, particularly hip openers, will be especially challenging and will require some patience and long-term practice. Everything suggested here is just a guideline. Come to know your students. Some students might be comfortable with this pose very early on, while for others it may take several years to get to Happy Baby pose. Either of these trajectories is fine, as long as the students are discovering what feels comfortable for them.

Another consideration under the exercises domain is your pace of instruction. In general, a slow pace to the presentation works better than a rapid pace. We are teaching folks to take some time with their bodies, and we do not want to rush them through it. There is also such a thing as too much time. Students may give you feedback that the holds are too long in certain positions, or that there is too much silence at times, and students may start to "space out." We need to be aware of finding a good rhythm where students can comprehend the material and feel at ease with it, without having the time to dissociate or drift off.

Our very first series of yoga classes at the Trauma Center occurred in 2003. There was no precedent, and we were truly going at it fresh for the first time. We decided that it would probably be a good idea to slow the pace of presentation down from the average yoga studio class, and we made a conscious attempt to do so. After class, almost every student mentioned that it was way too fast! This was an eye opener. This class was composed of a group of adult survivors of chronic childhood abuse and neglect. They felt completely rushed even though the instructor was consciously trying to slow everything down. They wanted a little more space to be in their bodies, to feel safe, and to have a mindful physical experience. We learned to slow it down even more.

The next piece of learning in this regard came during our pilot study of yoga for adult survivors of chronic childhood abuse. Students were so fidgety during Savasana that we were unable to use the physiological data—they had a sensor connected to their fingertips that measured heart rate, but they were twitching their fingers so much that the heart rate data were totally skewed. At that point, we were offering a silent Savasana for about three to five minutes. We shifted to a gentler guided body scan with only about a minute or two of total silence, and this seemed to work better at the Trauma Center. That said, some groups, like the adolescents we work with in residential schools, have enjoyed a longer, silent Savasana with some quiet music. For these groups, it is a time to rest that they may not get otherwise.

Distress tolerance is one skill that is developed through the use of yoga. This means that students are able to tolerate some minor discomfort without becoming triggered or overwhelmed. An important aspect of distress tolerance is having a sense of time. For many survivors, discomfort becomes intolerable because of thoughts such as, "This will never end" or "I can't stand it." It is important for the teacher to assist the students in creating a sense of time in which discomfort has a beginning and an end. Offering students a sense of predictability and control over their experience often helps them to tolerate uncomfortable sensations.

THE COUNTDOWN

For just about every yoga posture or exercise in our trauma-sensitive yoga classes, we use a technique called the *countdown*. Basically, this involves a slow, methodical count from three or five to zero that the teacher provides in order to give the postures a temporal frame and—important in the trauma context—to reassure students that the posture (the experience of the moment) has an end. For people with PTSD, the trauma is often experienced as ongoing. It continues to play itself out in the body, mind, and soul. When we ask folks to engage in sometimes-challenging breathing and moving exercises, it is quite possible that it will seem to our students that these challenges will never end, and they will understandably stop the exercise early on in order to avoid what they view as pain and suffering. For people with PTSD, a normal stimulus such as a challenging yoga form will often be interpreted as a traumatic event because the body is on high alert at all times and because the somatic discomfort is a reminder of traumatic experiences. We have found the countdown to be an effective way to reassure folks that the yoga posture will end and that we will move on to something else. We are providing folks with an opportunity to have an appropriately challenging (not harsh or painful) experience, and especially to notice that it begins and ends. It is our understanding that trauma survivors benefit from practicing the ending of appropriately challenging experiences in order to heal, and we get to do this many times within a yoga class. Teachers begin the countdown once all of the parameters of an exercise, and all of the choices available within the posture, have been explained.

Please note: We do not want people to hurt themselves or to engage in any yoga practice that is painful; therefore, we constantly qualify all of the postural cues with an instruction such as, "You are in control. If this is painful or uncomfortable for any reason, you can always stop what you are doing." While practicing the ending of appropriate challenges is good, it is equally important for trauma survivors to know that they do not have to engage in any yoga-related activity that causes them pain or suffering.

Experimenting with manageable distress tolerance can help students widen their window of tolerance for experience. Over time, this will help them to experience mildly uncomfortable or distressing emotional or physical sensations without shutting down or doing something to immediately stop the sensation. Uncomfortable emotions or physical sensations are often a source of information about what we need and what is not good for us. By building a tolerance for experiencing these sensations, students may eventually experience more confidence in setting limits on things that are not good for them and may have greater access to self-care.

Distress tolerance for manageable discomfort is one thing, but pain and injury are quite another. Some trauma survivors may feel that they have to follow the instructor's guidance and may push themselves past what is healthy. They may feel that they have to try the most challenging poses right away, and they may feel unsuccessful if they are unable to do the poses "correctly." These are big risk factors for injury. No matter what postures we are offering, we always want to give several options. For instance, we can offer the guidance, "If this doesn't work, try this or this." The constant is an instruction like, "If this is uncomfortable or painful to you for any reason, you can always come out of the posture and come back to your mindful breathing." We are teaching trauma survivors to identify what is happening in the moment in their bodies. If they detect pain on any level, we hope that they become willing and able to say, "No, I will not be in pain—my opinion about what is happening to me matters, and I can take control." These are "therapeutic moments" in your class that are extremely valuable. Let's design classes that give as many opportunities for this kind of experience as possible!

Responding to Triggered Reactions in a Yoga Class

At the Trauma Center Yoga Program, we have come to realize that our clients are being triggered all the time during the yoga classes. While this is the reality, we have also come to trust the yoga practice as a way for many trauma survivors to manage these triggers successfully.

For our clients, the world is full of triggers: cars backfire, sometimes people smell like sweat, sometimes people raise their voices, and so on. In this sense, the yoga room is no different—it is part of the world where triggers arise. In fact, it could be said that the yoga class may even up the ante in terms of triggers because we are working directly with the body, which is an extremely vulnerable realm for many trauma survivors.

While we recognize that triggers will naturally arise during a yoga class, we do believe that the trauma-sensitive yoga teacher has a special job that may be different from the job of a yoga teacher in other settings, and that is to be aware of the impact of triggers and to help participants utilize yoga techniques to manage some of these triggered reactions in the moment. If trauma survivors visit a medical doctor and ask for help managing triggers, they may be prescribed a medication; if they visit a clinician, they may be invited to process the experience;

if they visit a yoga teacher, we want to give them some yoga techniques that they can use for regulation.

What follows is an example from a Trauma Center yoga class that demonstrates how the yoga teacher offered a triggered student some yoga techniques to manage the experience.

COMING BACK TO MOUNTAIN

During a trauma-sensitive yoga class, the teacher noticed that a woman toward the front of the class began crying at a certain point. This student had been to the class regularly for many months. She had some familiarity with the room, the class, the teacher, and the other regular students. The teacher and student made eye contact, during which there was a shared sense that the student was OK and was managing her experience safely.

The teacher, however, kept a special eye on this student for the rest of the class. She noticed a few minutes later that the student stopped participating in the flow of the class and sat up with her hands over her heart (a gesture that the class had experimented with many times before). For the rest of the class, the woman would participate sporadically and then return to her seated position, with her hands over her heart, or experiment with Child's Pose. There was no further escalation in terms of symptoms.

At the end of the class, the teacher approached the student and acknowledged that she had noticed her crying and wanted to make sure she was OK. The student said that she felt flooded with emotion when the teacher said the word "pelvis" in relation to a particular exercise. She said that she was inclined, right that moment, to tell the teacher about her trauma history because it was all very overwhelming, and this may be a way for her to discharge the intensity.

At this point, the yoga teacher made a critical decision. She said that it would be fine for the student to talk about her trauma, but would she first like to experiment with standing up together in Mountain posture? "Yes, that sounds good," the student replied. It just so happened that this was enough in this case. This posture was very familiar to both teacher and student, something they had practiced together in the class context many times over the past several months. So they stood together in Mountain posture.

Next, the teacher invited the student, "Would you like to try breathing and moving together?" Again, the student said yes, so together they did some Sun Breaths, synchronizing their breaths and movements. For several minutes they practiced yoga together in this way. When the teacher brought it back to Mountain, they both paused together, smiled at each other, and the student said, "Yes, I'm good."

"Is there anything else that you need?" asked the teacher. The student asked if she could just sit quietly on her mat while the teacher cleaned up the room and prepared to leave.

After about ten minutes they said good night, and that was that. The teacher noticed a marked shift in the woman's energy from the heaviness as she had been saturated with emotion and wanted to talk about her trauma to a sense of lightness and ease after they had practiced a little yoga together.

Please note: The yoga teacher communicated that she was not afraid of hearing about the trauma, but still maintained her focus on how the student was doing. Witnessing the student's distress and helping her to regulate with yoga was enough for this student in this moment.

This story is an example of a yoga teacher offering a student some yoga techniques with which to manage a trigger. In this case, it worked very well. Using some familiar yoga practices, the student was able to ride out the trigger and move on. Please notice that she did not end up telling the yoga teacher about her trauma experience. Perhaps because she was at the Trauma Center where she went for psychotherapy, she felt at first that talking about her trauma was the best way for her to discharge some of the power of the triggered response. This may have worked for her as well; alternately, it could have led her to become flooded with traumatic material and left her with the added challenge of having to manage these exacerbated post-traumatic reactions effectively on her own until her next therapy appointment. As it was, the yoga practices clearly helped her find some immediate ease right in her body, and it was achieved without any verbal processing of her trauma narrative. We would like for yoga teachers and others to draw at least one conclusion from this story—that yoga techniques can be very effective at helping trauma survivors manage triggers when they arise. When triggers arise for your students, you can offer yoga techniques in good faith.

There were some other important factors involved that we think allowed the yoga teacher some space and confidence to do what she did. The teachers at the Trauma Center know that all students have a psychotherapist with whom they can process anything that arises in the yoga classes. Teachers also have a release to contact therapists and have done so on several occasions with concerns about a student's well-being. Also, this class took place at the Trauma Center, and the yoga teacher knew that if the situation were to become more of a crisis, there was a clinician in the building who could assist. Please be aware of these conditions for your students and have a sense of what kinds of safety nets they have around them.

Another important element of the example above is that the yoga practices the yoga teacher offered were very simple and very familiar to the student. When a student is in the midst of a trigger, it is not the time to teach something new. We recommend you have some core practices like the ones above that you can turn to in a crisis moment.

On one occasion, one of our students was visibly triggered at the end of a yoga class: stiffened body, rapid breath, tears in her eyes, and no eye contact. In this instance, the yoga teacher gently approached the student and was able to make eye contact and ask her if she was OK. The student responded that she was upset but that she was OK. The teacher felt like it was important to ask if the student had a plan for the evening. Did she have someone she could talk to? (Yes.) Did she have access to her therapist the next day if she felt it was necessary? (Yes.) In this case, the teacher took a few minutes to strategize with the student, recognizing that she was upset and acknowledging her concern for the student's safety. The yoga teacher was able to call the student's therapist the next day to alert her to the situation. Again, this demonstrates the power of teamwork at the Trauma Center: client, yoga teacher, and therapist are all working together toward the same goals. Recognizing both that yoga is very challenging for many trauma survivors, and also that it is part of the healing process, it is important for yoga instructors and clinicians to be informed about trauma and to be able to partner in this work.

If you decide to teach trauma-sensitive yoga classes, you will likely often witness students being triggered. The examples above are on the more intense end. Sometimes triggers come briefly during a class, and students are able to move though the experience by the end of class. We encourage you to begin to tune in to the body language of your students with a special eye toward some of the examples above, and also to know that this is very normal for a trauma-sensitive yoga class. Triggers will arise, and the yoga practices are what you have to offer. Many people have told us that these yoga techniques are some of the most effective trigger-management techniques that they have in their toolbox.

Conclusions

Experience is often our best teacher. Yoga students and practitioners have shared invaluable thoughts and insights with us over the years, based on their own experiences with the yoga classes and yoga-based exercises offered through our center. This email from a yoga student at the Trauma Center gets at the heart of the matter:

> Although I was really glad we had a class, I also liked talking with you about the trauma stuff and yoga. Coming to yoga as a trauma survivor was so hard for me, I like to think about ways to make some of that easier for other people. I really appreciated what was said in class about gestures today. Of course, in a way, it is all about the gestures, the open chest and shoulders or the closed ones. The act of opening my shoulders or my legs in Happy Baby pose [a yoga posture that involves being prone with the legs up in the air and the hips widened—a very open and exposed gesture] may be physical, but it also carries a lot of meaning. A lot of the meaning is rooted in my body, and that is what makes the gestures and just thinking about being able to do them so profound....
>
> For me it always comes back to the body and the memory that I store there.

Maybe because I was so young, I feel like the abuse lies deepest in a part of me that is fundamentally a physical being. So it is some of the seemingly most simple things, like just thinking that it is OK for me to breathe in and breathe out deeply, without fear. Because in some parts of my body, I still remember what it was like to be afraid to make noise breathing, and so that gesture of more open breathing is in and of itself profound. Same thing with Standing Mountain posture—there almost wouldn't need to be anything more than that. Except that I really do like feeling strong in my body; that makes me feel very safe, and so that part of yoga has become important to me too. Happy Baby right now is a gesture that is too open for me to make physically, but I can think about it, notice it. See you soon.

In a way this email perfectly sums up the entire idea of traumasensitive yoga that we have described in this book. This yoga student is recognizing the impact of the trauma on her body, and she is experimenting with postures and breath, while being fully present with that knowledge. She is assessing what works for her and what doesn't. She is making choices according to what "feels right" to her, and she is learning to trust those decisions and the information she is getting from her body. She is integrating breath and movement into her life in a safe, effective way and is curious about the process. Please note that this person had been practicing trauma-sensitive yoga for several years when she wrote these emails. Her insights are hard won, but we can all benefit from them.

We hope that this book has offered survivors, clinicians, and yoga teachers a framework for understanding the impact of trauma, as well as an appreciation of the important role of trauma-sensitive yoga in healing. Above all, we hope that survivors have found something useful in the text—something tangible that can be practiced. We encourage you to be creative, use what works, and put aside what does not seem helpful. Experiment, if you like, and decide for yourself.

Another survivor experimenting with yoga described her experience of coming alive again through her yoga practice. She recalled how she had felt dead, and her body was always cold and numb. She was disconnected from herself and isolated from other people. She began attending a trauma-sensitive yoga class and practiced yogabased strategies with her individual therapist to help her remain mindful in session and to work on regulating her emotions. After one particular session with her therapist in which she was practicing Seated Mountain and breathing exercises, she raised her head and looked her therapist in the eyes. She was present, experiencing the current moment, and she wasn't afraid of what she was feeling. She had tears in her eyes, and a big, warm smile broke out on her face. "I feel whole," she said.

Notes

ONE: RECLAIMING YOUR BODY

[1]   B.A. van der Kolk, "The Body Keeps the Score: Memory and the Evolving Psychobiology of Post Traumatic Stress," *Harvard Review of Psychiatry* 1, no.5 (1994): 253–265.

[2]   See U.S. Department of Health and Human Services, "The Fourth National Incidence Study of Childhood Abuse and Neglect" (2010), for an array of relevant statistics.

[3]   For a discussion on the impact of emotional neglect during childhood, see M. Blaustein and K. Kinniburgh, *Treating Traumatic Stress in Children and Adolescents* (New York: Guilford Press, 2010).

[4]   From a report by Dr. Bruce D. Perry, MD, PhD. Visit http://childtrauma academy.org/Documents/Prin_tcare_03_v2.pdf for more on this and other statistics related to childhood trauma.

[5]   For comprehensive reviews and comparison of the short-versus long-term effects of childhood abuse, see, for

example, J. Beitchman, K. Zucker, J. Hood, G. DaCosta, and D. Akman, "A Review of the Short-Term Effects of Child Sexual Abuse," *Child Abuse and Neglect* 15 (1991): 537–556; J. Beitchman, K. Zucker, J. Hood, G. DaCosta, D. Akman, and E. Cassavia, "A Review of the Long-Term Effects of Child Sexual Abuse," *Child Abuse and Neglect* 16 (1992): 101–118.

[6] Visit http://www.ojp.usdoj.gov/nij/topics/crime/intimate-partner-violence/extent.htm for this and other statistics related to trauma experienced by adults.

[7] Blaustein and Kinniburgh, *Treating Traumatic Stress,* 4.

[8] National Institute of Mental Health, "The Numbers Count: Mental Disorders in America." Many other relevant statistics are also presented in this paper.

[9] As a place to start your exploration of how trauma affects the brain, see B.A. van der Kolk, "Clinical Implications of Neuroscience Research," *Annals of the New York Academy of Sciences* 1071 (2006): 277–293. A meta-analysis of MRI studies examining the neuroanatomical differences in the brains of individuals with PTSD may also shed some light on the subject: A. Karl, M. Schaefer, L.S. Malta, et al., "A

Meta-analysis of Structural Brain Abnormalities in PTSD," *Neuroscience Biobehavioral Review* 30 (2006): 1004–1031.

[10] A good starting place for information on this topic is T. Luxenberg, J. Spinazzola, and B.A. van der Kolk, "Complex Trauma and Disorders of Extreme Stress (DESNOS) Diagnosis, Part I: Assessment," *Directions in Psychiatry* 21 (2001): 373–393. Another invaluable reference addressing the early impact of complex trauma is Cook et al., "Complex Trauma in Children and Adolescents," *Psychiatric Annals* 35, no.5 (2005): 390–398.

[11] The Adverse Childhood Experiences (ACE) Study, conducted by Felitti, Anda, and others, has resulted in numerous publications. One example is a 1998 article in the *Journal of Preventive Medicine* titled "Relationship of Childhood Abuse and Household Dysfunction to Many of the Leading Causes of Death in Adults." Visit the Centers for Disease Control website (www.cdc.gov) for more information.

[12] Along with Dr. Judith Herman's seminal book *Trauma and Recovery* (New York: Basic Books, 1992), another book that

explores the physicality of trauma in depth is Peter Levine's *Waking the Tiger* (Berkeley: North Atlantic Books, 1997).

[13]   P. Ogden and K. Minton, "Sensorimotor Psychotherapy: One Method for Processing Traumatic Memory," *Traumatology* 6, vol.3 (2000): 149–173. These authors have also written a book along with Clare Pain called *Trauma and the Body* (New York: W.W. Norton, 2006). Both works are deeply relevant to our topic.

TWO: TRAUMATIC STRESS

[1]   W.H.S. Jones, E.T. Withington, and P. Potter, eds. and trans., *Hippocrates, Works,* (London: Loeb Classical Library/Heinemann, 1923–88), 1:283. Extensive information about Hippocrates' theories is included in this six-volume work.

[2]   For a description of the historical basis of current understandings of emotions and mental health, see T. Brown, "Emotions and Disease in Historical Perspective," available at the National Library of Medicine's website, http://www.nlm.nih.go v/hmd/emotions/balance.html.

[3]   For a comprehensive overview of historical perspectives on hysteria, see M.S. Micale, *Approaching Hysteria: Disease and Its Interpretations.* (Princeton, NJ: Princeton University Press, 1995).

[4]   J.E. Erichsen, *On Railway and Other Injuries of the Nervous System* (London: Walton & Maberly, 1866).

[5]   J.M. Charcot, *Leçons sur les maladies du système nerveux faites à la Salpêtriére* (Paris: Bureaux du Progrès Médical, 1887).

[6]   C.G. Goetz, M. Bonduelle, and T. Gelfand, *Charcot: Constructing Neurology* (New York: Oxford University Press, 1995).

[7]   S. Freud, "The Aetiology of Hysteria," *The Standard Edition of the Complete Psychological Works of Sigmund Freud, Volume III (1893–1899): Early Psycho-Analytic Publications* (1896).

[8]   Abreactive techniques shared some similarities with exposure therapies in use today. These therapies appeal to some people's desires to "get it out" and "move on." However, as indicated in Van der Hart and Brown's 1992 paper (see note 9), "there exists a consensus at least among contemporary therapists of MPD and other post-traumatic states that abreaction alone and in itself is not

curative. Many of these patients regularly enter states during which they partially or completely reexperience trauma, without any resolution whatsoever."

[9]   For interesting reflections on Freud's concept of abreaction and its relevance for current-day treatment, see O. Van der Hart and P. Brown, "Abreaction Reevaluated," *Dissociation* 6, no.2/3 (1992): 162–180.

[10]   P. Janet, *Les medications psychologiques* (Paris: Felix Alcan, 1919). Reprint: Société Pierre Janet, Paris, 1984. English edition: *Psychological Healing* (New York: Arno Press, 1976).

[11]   For a review of the current relevance of Janet's theories, see P. Brown, O. van der Hart, and B.A. van der Kolk, "Pierre Janet and the Breakdown of Adaptation in Psychological Trauma," *American Journal of Psychiatry* 146, no.12 (1989): 1530–1540.

[12]   See note 9.

[13]   M. Stone, "Shellshock and the Psychologists," in *The Anatomy of Madness*, vol.2, eds. W.F. Bynum, R. Porter, and M. Shepherd (London: Tavistock, 1985), 242–271.

[14]   A. Kardiner, *The Traumatic Neurosis of War* (New York: Paul Hoeber, 1941).

[15]   J. Bremner, "Acute and Chronic Responses to Psychological Trauma: Where Do We Go from Here?" *American Journal of Psychiatry* 156 (1999): 349–351.

[16]   American Psychiatric Association, *Diagnostic and Statistical Manual of Mental Disorders*, 3rd ed. (Washington, DC: American Psychiatric Association, 1980).

[17]   See note 15.

[18]   A. Eftekhari, L.R. Stines, and L.A. Zoellner, "Do You Need to Talk about It? Prolonged Exposure for the Treatment of Chronic PTSD," *Behavior Analyst Today* 7, no.1 (2006): 70–83.

[19]   See E.B. Foa, E.A. Hembree, and B.O. Rothbaum, "Prolonged Exposure Therapy for PTSD: Emotional Processing of Traumatic Experiences; Therapist Guide," in *A Guide to Treatments That Work*, eds. P.E. Nathan and J.M. Gorman (New York: Oxford University Press, 2007). For a description of mechanisms of action of exposure therapy, see E.B. Foa and R.J. McNally, "Mechanisms of Change in Exposure Therapy," in *Current Controversies in the Anxiety Disorders*, ed.

R.M. Rapee (New York: Guilford Press, 1996), 329–343.

[20] P.A. Resick and M.K. Schnicke, *Cognitive Processing Therapy for Rape Victims* (London: Sage Publications, 1996).

[21] Each of these treatment modalities, including the CBT-based interventions mentioned, receive extensive review and comparative examination of merit in the Practice Guidelines developed by the International Society for Traumatic Stress Studies. E. Foa, T. Keane, M. Friedman, and J. Cohen, eds., *Effective Treatments for PTSD: Practice Guidelines from the International Society for Traumatic Stress Studies* (New York: Guilford Press, 2009).

[22] S. Benish, Z. Imel, and B. Wampold, "The Relative Efficacy of Bona Fide Psychotherapies for Treating Post-traumatic Stress Disorder: A Meta-analysis of Direct Comparisons," *Clinical Psychology Review* 28 (2008): 746–758.

[23] T. Luxenberg, J. Spinazzola, and B.A. van der Kolk, "Complex Trauma and Disorders of Extreme Stress (DESNOS) Diagnosis, Part I: Assessment," *Directions in Psychiatry* 21: 373–393.

[24]   E.B. Foa, T. Keane, and M. Friedman, eds., *Treatment Guidelines for Posttraumatic Stress Disorder* (New York: Guilford Press, 2000).

[25]   C.B. Becker, C. Zayfert, and E. Anderson surveyed close to a thousand doctoral-level psychologists in their 1994 study, "A Survey of Psychologists' Attitudes towards and Utilization of Exposure Therapy for PTSD," *Behavior Research and Therapy* 42 (1994): 277–292. They found that although most clinicians reported familiarity with exposure therapy, a small minority used it in their clinical practices. They expressed a number of concerns about barriers to the use of exposure therapy, including concerns that clients' symptoms such as substance abuse and suicidal ideation would increase, as well as concerns about therapy dropout. For more information on this issue, see also J.A. Jaeger, A. Echiverri, L.A. Zoellner, L. Post, and N.C. Feeny, "Factors Associated with Choice of Exposure Therapy for PTSD," *International Journal of Behavioral Consultation and Therapy* 5, no.2 (2009): 294–310.

[26] For a careful empirical investigation and critique of the generalizability of PTSD treatment outcome literature, see J. Spinazzola, M. Blaustein, and B.A. van der Kolk, "Posttraumatic Stress Disorder Treatment Outcome Research: The Study of Unrepresentative Samples," *Journal of Traumatic Stress*, 18, no.5 (2005): 425–436.

[27] Ibid.

[28] M. Cloitre, L. Cohen, and K. Koenan, *Treating Survivors of Childhood Abuse: Psychotherapy for the Interrupted Life* (New York: Guilford Press, 2006).

[29] See M.M. Linehan and L. Dimeff, "Dialectical Behavior Therapy in a Nutshell," *California Psychologist* 34 (2001): 10–13. For a more complete review of DBT, see Linehan's 1993 manual: M.M. Linehan, *Skills Training Manual for Treatment of Borderline Personality Disorder* (New York: Guilford Press, 1993).

[30] For a description of EMDR, see Francine Shapiro's work: F. Shapiro, "Efficacy of the Eye Movement Desensitization Procedure in the Treatment of Traumatic Memories," *Journal of Traumatic Stress* 2 (1989): 199–223; F. Shapiro, "Eye Movement Desensitization:

A New Treatment for Post-traumatic Stress Disorder," *Journal of Behavior Therapy and Experimental Psychiatry* 20 (1989): 211–217; F. Shapiro, "Eye Movement Desensitization and Reprocessing: Basic Principles, Protocols, and Procedures" (New York: Guilford Press, 1995).

[31] For a description of resource installation protocols for use with EMDR, see Debbie Korn and Andrew Leed's work: D.L. Korn and A.M. Leeds, "Preliminary Evidence of Efficacy for EMDR Resource Development and Installation in the Stabilization Phase of Treatment of Complex Posttraumatic Stress Disorder," *Journal of Clinical Psychology* 58, no.12 (2002): 1465–1487.

[32] For a delineation of the core components of treatment with complexly traumatized children and description of several of the emerging models for use with this population, see Cook et al., "Complex Trauma in Children and Adolescents," *Psychiatric Annals* 35, no.5 (2005): 390–398. Among these models, the Attachment, Regulation, and Competency (ARC) framework is particularly noteworthy: M. Blaustein and

K. Kinniburgh, *Treating Traumatic Stress in Children and Adolescents* (New York: Guilford Press, 2010); also see K. Kinniburgh, M. Blaustein, J. Spinazzola, and B.A. van der Kolk, "Attachment, Self-regulation and Competency: A Comprehensive Framework for Children with Complex Trauma," *Psychiatric Annals* 35, no.5 (2005): 424–430.

[33]   B.A. van der Kolk, "Clinical Implications of Neuroscience Research in PTSD," *Annals of the New York Academy of Sciences* (2006): 1–17.

[34]   P. Ogden and K. Minton, "Sensorimotor Psychotherapy: One Method for Processing Traumatic Memory," *Traumatology* 6, no.3 (2000). See also P. Ogden, K. Minton, and C. Pain, *Trauma and the Body* (New York: W.W. Norton, 2006).

[35]   See note 33.

[36]   See M.J. Nijsen, G. Croiset, M. Diamant, R. Stam, D. Delsing, D. de Wied, and V.M. Wiegant, "Conditioned Fear-Induced Tachycardia in the Rat: Vagal Involvement," *European Journal of Pharmacology* 350, no.2–3 (1998): 211–222. In this study, rats in a conditioned fear condition (being placed

in a cage where they had previously received electroshocks) showed an increase in both adrenaline and noradrenaline (activation of the SNS), as well as immobility and decreased tachycardia (indications of activation of the PNS).

[37]   Stephen Porges has postulated that there are two vagal systems that are neuroanatomically different and that represent different adaptive strategies: the vegetative vagus, which is responsible for passive, reflex-based regulation of visceral functions, and the smart vagus, which is associated with more active regulatory systems such as attention, emotion, and communication. See S. Porges, "Orienting in a Defensive World: Mammalian Modification of Our Evolutionary Heritage; A Polyvagal Theory," *Psychophysiology* 32 (1995): 301–318.

[38]   E.D. Abercrombie and B.L. Jacobs, "Systemic Naloxone Administration Potentiates Locus Coeruleus Noradrenergic Neuronal Activity under Stressful but Not Non-stressful Conditions," *Brain Research* 441 (1988): 362–366. Also see B.D. Perry, R.A.

Pollard, T.L. Blakley, W.L. Baker, and D. Vigilante, "Childhood Trauma, the Neurobiology of Adaptation and Use-Dependent Development of the Brain: How States become Traits," *Infant Mental Health Journal* 16, no.4 (1995): 271–291.

[39]   Rachel Yehuda has done a great deal of work on the physiological basis of PTSD, particularly focusing on the stress hormone cortisol. For instance, see R. Yehuda and A.C. McFarlane, "Conflict between Current Knowledge about Posttraumatic Stress Disorder and Its Original Conceptual Basis," *American Journal of Psychiatry* 152, no.12 (1995): 1705–1713.

[40]   J. Herman, *Trauma and Recovery* (New York: Basic Books, 1992).

[41]   B.A. van der Kolk, "The Body Keeps the Score," *Harvard Review of Psychiatry* 1 (1994): 253–265.

[42]   O. van der Hart, B.A. van der Kolk, and S. Boon, "Treatment of Dissociative Disorders," in *Trauma, Memory, and Dissociation*, eds. J.D. Bremner and C.R. Marmar (Washington, DC: American Psychiatric Press, 1998), 253–283.

[43]   See note 40.

[44] For instance, see the *Psychotherapy Networker* article on Bessel A. van der Kolk: M. Sykes Wylie, "The Limits of Talk: Bessel van der Kolk Wants to Transform the Treatment of Trauma," *Psychotherapy Networker* 28, no.1 (2004): 30–41. Pat Ogden and others at the Hakomi Institute hold similar views. See, for instance, P. Ogden, K. Minton, and C. Pain, *Trauma and the Body* (New York: W.W. Norton, 2006).

THREE: YOGA

[1] V. Scaravelli, *Awaking the Spine: The Stress-Free New Yoga That Works with the Body to Restore Health, Vitality, and Energy* (New York: Harper One, 1991).

[2] For a detailed exploration of the history of yoga, see G. Feuerstein, *The Yoga Tradition* (Prescott, AZ: Hohm Press, 1998).

[3] Patanjali, *The Yoga-Sutra of Patañjali: A New Translation and Commentary*, trans. G. Feuerstein (Rochester, VT: Inner Traditions, 1989).

[4] For a detailed examination of how the guru tradition may be manipulated by individuals and the kind of interpersonal

damage that can ensue as a result, readers are directed to G. Falk, *Stripping the Gurus: Sex, Violence, Abuse, and Enlightenment* (Toronto: Million Monkeys Press, 2009). It is also appropriate to note that any systems that are predicated around deeply held and indisputable beliefs, powerful and compelling leaders, and inadequate monitoring and regulation of leaders' exercise of power can be abused, such as was observed in the late-twentiethcentury revelations of sexual abuse within the Catholic Church. Though the guru tradition per se is not always explicitly named in such contexts, similar power dynamics between "masters" and "students" are often evident. Another important reference here is to the "cult of personality" that revolves around many of the well-known yoga teachers in the West, and to the potential threat to the integrity and intent of yoga practice when one individual comes to dominate a segment of the "yoga market." Accordingly, readers are cautioned and encouraged to conduct consumer research in the selection of a yoga school just as carefully as they would in the selection of a treatment center or psychotherapist.

[5]   The magazine *Yoga Journal* often does a survey of the yoga market that investigates some aspects of the business side of yoga. Results from years past can be found in print and online.

[6]   Bikram yoga, commonly known as hot yoga, is a system of yoga developed by Bikram Choudhury and popularized in the 1970s. More information can be found at http://www.bikramyoga.com.

[7]   Power yoga is a Western adaptation of yoga that focuses on strength and flexibility. It is a Vinyasa style of yoga that is used by many Western students as a form of exercise and fitness.

[8]   More information on Iyengar yoga can be found on B.K. S Iyengar's website, http://www.bksiyengar.com.

[9]   Vinyasa-style yoga is one of the most commonly practiced forms of yoga in the West. It emphasizes the connection between postures, or asanas, and breath. It is sometimes referred to as flow yoga.

[10]   Our intention is not to condemn popularized forms of yoga in the West, nor to suggest that some trauma survivors have not walked into a public yoga studio and had a great, healing experience, but rather to highlight the

many potential pitfalls that are so common wherever yoga is being practiced publicly so that readers can become a bit more mindful about the whole process and make choices that they deem appropriate.

FOUR: TRAUMA-SENSITIVE YOGA

[1]   See B.A. van der Kolk, "The Body Keeps the Score," *Harvard Review of Psychiatry* 1 (1994): 253–265. This article is also included in B.A. van der Kolk et al., *Traumatic Stress* (New York: Guilford Press, 2006). The whole book is a rich trove of information on the topic of trauma and its impact on the entire organism.

[2]   For the purpose of our book we use a working definition of "self-regulation" that refers to "the ability to restore a state of calmness or self-control to one's thoughts, emotions and body when triggered or distressed." We are interested in helping trauma survivors find effective ways to use their body and breathing to achieve this and other expressions of self-regulation when they

want or need to do so. We will explore this theme many times throughout the book.

[3] This comes from the introduction that Bessel A. van der Kolk wrote for Ogden, Minton, and Pain's *Trauma and the Body*.

[4] Some articles that examine thinking and research around how trauma survivors might be stuck in the past and be unable to fully experience the present include: T. Luxenberg, J. Spinazzola, and B.A. van der Kolk, "Complex Trauma and Disorders of Extreme Stress (DESNOS) Diagnosis, Part I: Assessment," *Directions in Psychiatry* 21 (2001): 373–393; T. Luxenberg, J. Spinazzola, J. Hidalgo, C. Hunt, and B.A. van der Kolk, "Complex Trauma and Disorders of Extreme Stress (DESNOS) Diagnosis, Part II: Treatment," *Directions in Psychiatry* 21 (2001): 395–415; B.A. van der Kolk, S. Roth, D. Pelcovitz, S. Sunday, and J. Spinazzola, "Disorders of Extreme Stress: The Empirical Foundation of a Complex Adaptation to Trauma," *Journal of Traumatic Stress* 18, no.5 (2005): 389–399.

[5] Model Mugging is a self-defense course that is based on martial arts. Using padded trainers to simulate assaults, it teaches

people to defend themselves against assailants who may or may not be armed. For more information, see http://www.mo delmugging.org.

[6]   A. Cook, J. Spinazzola, J. Ford, C. Lanktree, M. Blaustein, M. Cloitre, R. DeRosa, R. Hubbard, R. Kagan, J. Liataud, K. Mallah, E. Olafson, and B.A. van der Kolk, "Complex Trauma in Children and Adolescents," *Psychiatric Annals* 35, no.5 (2005): 390–398.

[7]   See M. Blaustein and K. Kinniburgh, *Treating Traumatic Stress in Children and Adolescents* (New York: Guilford Press, 2010).

[8]   Bessel A. van der Kolk, in his paper "Clinical Implications of Neuroscience Research," mentions the "failures of attention and memory in posttraumatic stress disorder (PTSD)" that "interfere with the [survivor's] capacity to engage in the present." This, he continues, can result in traumatized individuals "los[ing] their way in the world." This is what we are getting at when we attempt to reconnect with a sense of rhythm and purpose using yoga.

SIX: FOR CLINICIANS

[1]   Mindfulness is based in Buddhist meditation practices. It was brought to the West by teachers such as Thich Nhat Hanh and popularized by Jon Kabat-Zinn and others. Thich Nhat Hanh is a Vietnamese Buddhist monk and author who has written multiple books on mindfulness, including his 1991 book, *Miracle of Mindfulness*, his 1992 book, *Peace Is Every Step: The Path of Mindfulness in Everyday Life*, and his 1999 book, *The Miracle of Mindfulness: A Manual on Meditation*. Jon Kabat-Zinn is an emeritus professor of medicine and founder of the Stress Reduction Clinic at the University of Massachusetts Medical School. He has written multiple works on mindfulness, including his well-known 1994 book, *Wherever You Go, There You Are: Mindfulness Meditation in Everyday Life*.

[2]   Distress tolerance is one of the basic skills learned in dialectical behavior therapy (DBT). DBT was originally developed for clients diagnosed with borderline personality disorder, but we view the skills as central to individuals who are dealing with complex trauma responses. See Marsha Linehan's 1993 treatment manual,

Skills Training Manual for Treatment of Borderline Personality Disorder, for a further description of the skills involved in DBT.

[3] The term *window of tolerance* was coined by Dan Siegel and was used by Pat Ogden in developing her modulation model. This terminology is now common among clinicians and researchers who are addressing issues of dysregulation in individuals suffering from complex trauma. D. Siegel, *The Developing Mind: Toward a Neurobiology of Interpersonal Experience* (New York: Guilford Press, 1999).

[4] In fact, the name of one form of yoga, Vinyasa, actually means "breath-synchronized movement."

[5] M. Csikszentmihalyi, *Flow: The Psychology of Optimal Experience* (New York: Harper and Row, 1990). In this book, Csikszentmihalyi refers to flow as being a state of complete absorption and engagement with an activity at hand. He believes that people are most happy when they are in a state of flow.

[6] J. Herman, *Trauma and Recovery* (New York: Basic Books, 1992), 133.

seven: FOR YOGA TEACHERS

[1]   This book is not intended to teach anyone how to be a yoga teacher. Our intention is to help certified yoga teachers become more trauma-sensitive. For information about becoming a yoga teacher, visit http ://www.yogaalliance.org.

About the Authors

A registered yoga teacher, David Emerson is the director of yoga services at the Trauma Center at Justice Resource Institute in Brookline, Massachusetts. In 2003 he collaborated with Bessel van der Kolk, MD, the founder and medical director of the Trauma Center, to create the Trauma Center Yoga Program, which includes classes and teacher training programs. Emerson currently leads trainings for yoga teachers and clinicians interested in offering trauma-sensitive yoga to their clients.

Elizabeth Hopper, PhD, is a licensed clinical psychologist with a specialization in traumatic stress and has worked with trauma survivors for the past fourteen years. She is a staff psychologist, supervisor, and the associate director of training at the Trauma Center at Justice Resource Institute. Dr. Hopper is also the director of Project REACH, a program that serves survivors of human trafficking throughout the United States. She offers national training and consultation on traumatic stress and alternative interventions for trauma survivors.

Back Cover Material

"**AT LAST,** an engaging, accessible, theoretically grounded guide for the safe and effective use of yoga to heal from trauma! With a rich understanding of both the practice of yoga and the legacy of trauma, the authors skillfully weave together theory, research, mindfulness, case vignettes, yoga instruction, and more into a clear and compelling argument for reclaiming the body through their 'trauma-sensitive' modified yoga. Innovative and practical, this book is an indispensable resource for traumatized individuals, yoga teachers, clinicians, and anyone else who is looking to rediscover the natural intelligence of the body."

–**Pat Ogden, PhD,** founder of the Sensorimotor Psychotherapy Institute and author of *Trauma and the Body: A Sensorimotor Approach to Psychotherapy*

"The trauma-sensitive yoga program developed by the authors through practical and clinical experience incorporates the best that yoga has to offer with what will benefit trauma patients safely and comfortably."

–**Sat Bir Singh Khalsa, PhD,** Assistant Professor of Medicine at Harvard Medical School and Director of Research for the Kundalini Research Institute

Trauma survivors—whether from abuse, accident, or war—can end up deeply and profoundly wounded, betrayed by their body for failing to get them to safety and for causing them pain. To fully heal from trauma, a connection must be made to oneself, including one's body. *Overcoming Trauma through Yoga* introduces trauma-sensitive yoga, a modified yoga program developed at the Trauma Center at Justice Resource Institute. Expanding beyond traditional talk therapies that only focus on the mind, trauma-sensitive yoga allows trauma survivors to cultivate a more positive relationship with their bodies through mindfulness, breathing, and gentle yoga exercises. The book provides an in-depth description of post-traumatic stress disorder (PTSD), explores the four key characteristics of trauma-sensitive yoga, and presents a trauma-sensitive yoga practice sequence that can be incorporated by home practitioners, yoga teachers, and therapists. Recommendations for integrating yoga-based interventions into therapy and suggestions for building a trauma-sensitive yoga class are rounded out by valuable case stories.

A

Abreaction, *16, 21*

Action, taking effective, *76, 78, 80*

Adverse Childhood Experiences (ACE) study, *6*

Affect regulation, *171, 173, 174*

Assists, *49, 92, 94, 195, 196, 198, 200, 201*

B

Balance, *166*

Belly breathing, *151, 185*

Bikram yoga, *44, 46*

Boat posture, *131, 134*

Body,
    changing relationship with, *159, 161, 163*
    disconnection from, *34, 36, 176, 177, 179*
    listening to, *75*

Breathing,

affect regulation and, *173, 174*
awareness of, *62*
belly, *151, 185*
integrating movement and, *177, 179*
nasal, *156*
ratio, *151*

Bridge posture, *125, 126, 128*

Buddhism, *40*

C

Cat Tilts, *111, 112*

Centering, *151, 163, 164, 166, 167*

Chair posture, *120, 124*

Child abuse,
    centering and, *164*
    effects of, *6*

Child's Pose, *107, 108, 111, 151, 217*

Child's Pose Side Stretch, *111*

www.ingramcontent.com/pod-product-compliance
Lightning Source LLC
Chambersburg PA
CBHW010142270326
41929CB00021B/3342

* 9 7 8 1 0 3 8 7 5 8 0 2 6 *